psst... come this way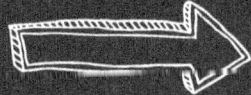

... my very first cookbook :-)

I'M SO EXCITED TO SHARE MY **passion** FOR FOOD WITH YOU...
COME ON NOW... GRAB AN APRON...

&

...LET'S GET **cooking!**

Till the next time!

welcome to MY TABLE

by

siba

MTONGANA

contents

What to expect inside... please come on a journey with me...

HOW TO USE THE QR CODES

One of the brilliant features of this cookbook are the QR codes that enable you to watch quick videos of me making the recipes. To use them, just follow these easy steps:

1. Download a QR code reader to your smartphone from an app store.
2. Open the QR code reader and hold your phone over a code – it must be clearly visible on your smartphone's screen. Your phone will either scan the code automatically or you'll be prompted to take a snap of it.
3. Your smartphone will then navigate you to the video.

Note, some recipe preparations and presentations vary slightly from those in the book.

look, daddy, this is how you do it!

its a family affair !

my story...

once upon

A THYME...

One of my early memories is of sitting at our kitchen table at home, watching my mother make umphokoqo, a light, crumbly mealie porridge. She took a pinch of salt, weighed it in her hand and added it to the water. When I asked how she measured the salt, she shrugged and said, 'You just feel it with your hand.'

It was the kind of answer my mother typically gave, drawing on experience and the accumulated knowledge and wisdom of all the women who came before her. There are some things she just knew. That's why we called her Mthombo wo lwazi, the well of wisdom.

I think this was how cooking captured my heart. Although I did not think of it in so many words, then, I was fascinated by the strange intertwining of chemistry and instinct that reigned in a kitchen. I wanted to know how my mother did it and I wanted to do it too.

We cooked traditional food at home – always rice or samp and beans, meat, gravy and at least three vegetables. But don't be fooled, these simple ingredients saw so many new variations and twists that it was easily possible to believe that my mother was a magician.

This is really the crux of it: food is all about family and friends, and putting your heart into preparing a meal is the same as presenting

i ♥ food

them with a wonderful gift. Food prepared with care says, 'I love you', and tastes even better when shared with our nearest and dearest.

I grew up in Mdantsane, a township outside East London, in a large family – I am the youngest of six children, plus two adopted, which makes us eight – deeply rooted in the Christian tradition of giving and sharing. My mom, Noliza Mnwana, a teacher, was big on education. She constantly reminded us that lilifa lethu, it's our true inheritance, that no one can take away from us. My father, Mncedisi Mnwana, who was a supervisor at a leather goods manufacturing company, was concerned with finding peace and meaning in one's life.

AS A TEENAGER, I REGULARLY COOKED OUR FAMILY MEALS

As a teenager, I regularly cooked our family meals. My parents were intrigued by my enthusiasm, but were a little shocked when I broke the news that I was planning a career in the food industry. My mother, especially, thought that it could mean only one thing: cooking for a white madam in a suburban kitchen somewhere. Celebrity and TV chefs hadn't really arrived in South Africa yet.

My father, who knew that I was passionate about food, was more sympathetic. He believed that it was important for me to study something I loved doing. That way, he said, I would never feel I was working and things would just flow and be easy. His mediation persuaded my mother to let me do my Food and Consumer Sciences degree at the Cape Peninsula University of Technology in Cape Town in 2003. I majored in Food, Food Science and Nutrition. This comforted my mom as she felt that studying the theory of nutrition would come in handy once I had kids. They're both extremely proud of

P.T.O

ukupheka = cooking

my achievements so far; and are relieved that allowing me to follow my passion has turned out better than they could have dreamt.

I met my husband, Brian Mtongana, while studying in Cape Town. It was the beginning of a life-long friendship, partnership and love affair – even if my parents did make him wait seven years to marry me! He has been my biggest supporter from my early days as an assistant lecturer at university, during my time as a food editor, my first and subsequent TV shows and now, most importantly, in publishing this book. He has contributed massively to achieving this shared dream. And, best of all, we have two boys – Lonwabo and Linamandla – the crowning glory of our lives. And, letting you in on a secret, we have a little girl on the way!

My palate has evolved over the years, flirting with a range of local and global trends as they appear and fade again. Travelling has exposed me to so many wonderful flavours and ideas, many of which pop up over and over in my recipes. Traditional fare has also retained a strong presence; and my three boys' tastes are also a strong influence. Brian is a great sounding board. When I try something new and ask his opinion, he'll be kind but totally honest.

FOOD SHOULD BE BEAUTIFUL AND TASTY, BUT EASY TO MAKE

Whatever the style or taste, my overriding concern is convenience. I believe food should be beautiful and tasty, but easy to make. I don't want to intimidate people by using 'in' terms and phrases. I want to show people how to make dinner in no time; and I want to provide the kind of tips that will make something you whipped up in under an hour look like you've been slaving over the stove all day.

You'll always find tinned tomatoes and a variety of tinned beans, pastes, rice, maize meal and lots of veggies in my pantry. With these basic ingredients, you can produce so many awesome dishes in almost no time.

As a mother and wife, I often think about health and nutrition. It is a truism that our eating habits affect our health, state of mind and longevity, yet the prevalence of obesity, diabetes and heart disease continues to rise. As I see it, my challenge is to create recipes and menus that delight all our senses but are also nutritious. Instinctively, I feel that my mom's emphasis on vegetables in our diet at home was right, which is why you'll find a lot of greens and low GI foods in my recipes. But, I am by no means rigid in my approach. A slice of cake or a wonderful dessert now and again can do wonders for one's mood. I guess the old adage that prescribes moderation in everything still holds true.

In our household, Sunday mornings are church and family time, followed by the traditional feast. You'll find some of my favourites in the meat and fish sections. We're also great salad eaters as you'll see from my salads and sides section. They're all incredibly easy to make and take very little time. I hope that you'll be inspired to put on that apron and get busy in your kitchen. Jazz it up, experiment and share with friends. This is my gift to you!

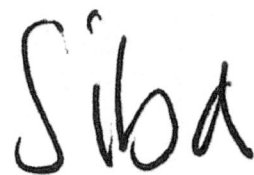

Breakfast and brunch are a sign that the day has just begun and great things are about to happen!

breakfast, BRUNCH, LUNCH & CANAPÉS

WEEKEND GRANOLA

THIS IS MY ALL-TIME FAVOURITE GRANOLA RECIPE. IT ALWAYS WORKS AND IT'S EVERYTHING I EXPECT A GRANOLA TO BE: CRUNCHY, WONDERFULLY AROMATIC — THE SMELL OF CINNAMON WAFTS THROUGH THE HOUSE WHILE IT'S BAKING — AND ABSOLUTELY DELICIOUS. WE LIVE SUCH BUSY LIVES AND WE'RE NOT ALWAYS ABLE TO HAVE BREAKFAST TOGETHER AS A FAMILY, BUT ON WEEKENDS WE GO ALL OUT AND, WHETHER FOR BREAKFAST OR BRUNCH, THIS IS ON THE MENU.

PREPARATION TIME: 10 MIN
BAKING TIME: 25 MIN
COOKING TIME: 5 MIN
MAKES 1,5-LITRE JAR

250ml oats
110ml desiccated coconut
40ml wheat germ
110ml pumpkin seeds
60ml sunflower seeds
50g whole raw almonds
50g whole Brazil nuts
50g whole pecan nuts
5ml ground cinnamon
100ml dried cranberries
60ml banana chips

SYRUP
60ml dark brown sugar
90ml butter
180ml honey
2ml vanilla extract

SERVE WITH
berry sauce (see page 199 for recipe)
and plain yoghurt, to taste

METHOD

Preheat the oven to 180°C and lightly grease a baking tray with butter. Place the oats, desiccated coconut, wheat germ, pumpkin and sunflower seeds, Brazil and pecan nuts, and almonds in the baking tray along with the cinnamon and mix well.

Bake in the oven for 15 minutes until crispy and slightly golden. In the meantime, make the syrup: heat the sugar, butter and honey in a saucepan for 5 minutes, stirring until well combined and slightly thickened. Remove from the heat and add the vanilla extract.

Remove the toasted mix from the oven and pour the syrup over it, mixing until all the ingredients are coated in the syrup.

Return to the oven and bake for a further 10 minutes until golden brown. Remove from the oven and leave to cool slightly before adding the dried cranberries and banana chips.

Allow to cool completely before placing into a sealable, clean storage jar. Serve the granola with a berry compote and plain yoghurt or a bit of milk if you prefer. It's also nice as a snack.

SCAN TO WATCH
A VIDEO ON
HOW TO
MAKE THIS RECIPE

Siba's tip...
It can keep in a jar for up to 3 weeks as long as it has cooled down completely and been sealed well.

CAPE TOWN TARTS

When I don't have much time to spend on making breakfast, this is my go-to recipe. Once all the ingredients are prepped, it's a matter of mixing everything into a jug, lining each muffin tin with the prosciutto and pouring the mixture over it. Then letting the oven do the cooking while carrying on with other things!

METHOD

Preheat the oven to 180°C. Line a 12-hole muffin tin with one slice of prosciutto in each hole, making sure to cover the bases and sides.

Heat the oil and sauté the onion for 4 minutes until soft and translucent, and place aside to cool. Mix with the tomatoes, blue cheese, olives and chives. Divide into the prepared bases.

In a jug, whisk the eggs and milk together and add a pinch of salt and black pepper. Pour equal amounts into the prepared mixture and sprinkle with the Parmesan.

Bake in the oven for 15 minutes or until puffed up and set. Cool for a few minutes and gently remove from the muffin tin.

PREPARATION TIME: 15 MIN
BAKING TIME: 20 MIN
MAKES 12

12 slices prosciutto
15ml olive oil
2 medium red onions,
very thinly sliced
150g red and yellow baby plum
tomatoes, quartered
50g mild blue cheese,
cut into pieces
75ml pitted black
olives, chopped
60ml chives, chopped
6 large eggs
225ml milk
salt and freshly ground
black pepper
30ml Parmesan cheese,
finely grated

SCAN TO WATCH
A VIDEO ON
HOW TO
MAKE THIS RECIPE

BREAKFAST FLAPJACKS*

I LEARNT TO DO FLAPJACKS FOR BREAKFAST LATER IN LIFE BECAUSE BREAKFAST WAS USUALLY HOMEMADE MAIZE MEAL PORRIDGE OR OATS. OTHER COOKED PORRIDGES APPEARED ONCE IN A BLUE MOON. AT WEEKENDS WE SOMETIMES HAD CEREAL, FOLLOWED BY AN EGG BREAKFAST AND BOEREWORS (SAUSAGE), TOMATO RELISH (THAT WE CALLED BISTO) WITH BREAD. BEING A MOM, I EXPERIMENT A LOT IN THE KITCHEN AND THIS SO HAPPENS TO BE SOMETHING THAT LONWABO AND I ENJOY DOING AND EATING TOGETHER — SO DOES BRIAN — USUALLY ON WEEKENDS. I OFTEN PUT LONWABO ON THE KITCHEN COUNTER AND HE HELPS ME WHISK THE PANCAKE BATTER. IT'S ONE OF OUR MANY SPECIAL BONDING TIMES IN THE KITCHEN.

PREPARATION TIME: 15 MIN
COOKING TIME: 10 MIN
SERVES 4–6

250ml all-purpose flour
30ml white sugar
10ml baking powder
2ml salt
150g fresh blueberries
1 egg
15ml butter, melted
250ml milk
20ml canola oil

SERVE WITH
60ml honey
50g blueberries
100g strawberries, sliced
or halved
plain yoghurt, to taste

METHOD

In a large bowl, combine the dry ingredients (flour, sugar, baking powder and salt). Mix in the blueberries and make a well in the centre.

In a jug, whisk the egg, melted butter and milk together, and pour into the hollowed centre, gently stirring to combine. Be careful not to over mix – it's okay to have a few lumps.

Heat a large non-stick frying pan until hot and brush with the oil. Add three tablespoons of the batter and level lightly using the back of a spoon. Cook until a few bubbles show on top. Turn and cook for 2 minutes on the other side.

Set aside and continue until the batter is used up. Plate and serve with a drizzle of honey, extra blueberries, strawberries and plain yoghurt.

Flapjacks are called pancakes in the US and crumpets in some countries.

Siba's tip...
If you prefer more than a drizzle of honey to sweeten your pancake, add an extra 15–30ml of sugar to the dry ingredients. To test if a flipped pancake has cooked long enough, lightly press the thickest part of it with your finger and it should spring up without leaving a dent. Place the pancakes on a cooling rack rather than a plate to prevent them from becoming soggy underneath.

this lovely dressing amplifies the glorious flavours of this dish!

BAKED STUFFED PROSCIUTTO + CAMEMBERT FIGS

I LOVE FIGS, ESPECIALLY WRAPPED IN PROSCIUTTO AND MY FAVOURITE CHEESE, CAMEMBERT. THIS COMBINATION REALLY IS LOVELY WHETHER SLIGHTLY GRILLED FOR 5 MINUTES TO LIGHTLY MELT THE CHEESE OR EATEN JUST AS IS, WITHOUT GRILLING, BUT THEN I ADD A FEW WILD ROCKET LEAVES TO EACH ONE AND MUNCH MY WAY TO GRATIFICATION, WHICH OFTEN MEANS INDULGENCE!

PREPARATION TIME: 10 MIN
BAKING TIME: 5 MIN
SERVES 4

400g (8) black figs, quartered
½ wheel Camembert, halved
and sliced
140g prosciutto slices,
halved lengthways

DRESSING
100g (2) fig pulp
60ml extra virgin olive oil
45ml rice wine vinegar
2 drops of honey

METHOD

Quarter the top half of the figs, leaving the bottom half intact, and press the sides of each so you can see more of the flesh. Place a slice of cheese in each centre and top with prosciutto.

Place on a lightly greased baking tray and grill at 230°C for 3–5 minutes, until the cheese melts. Remove and place on a platter.

Mix the dressing ingredients together and pour onto the platter over the figs.

Siba's tip...

As a smaller canapé, you could quarter the figs all the way down and then bundle each quarter, along with a slice of Camembert cheese and a few wild rocket leaves, into a piece of prosciutto cut in half lengthways. Add a wooden cocktail skewer to each to make them easy to hold and eat as nibbles. They're also great drizzled with a bit of balsamic vinegar dressing.

WARM MARKET SALAD

On Saturday mornings, I love going to the food market and getting fresh produce from local farmers and vendors. The quality of the produce is always great, and I often go early to miss the buzz and be back in time to prepare brunch for visiting friends. I like hosting a brunch because it's a two-in-one affair (breakfast and lunch at the same time) and doesn't take longer than 3 hours, giving me time to catch up with friends and still have the rest of the day to spend with my little ones.

PREPARATION TIME: 15 MIN
COOKING TIME: 20 MIN
SERVES 4

140g asparagus, thoroughly rinsed and woody ends trimmed
1 red onion, quartered (optional)
5ml fresh garlic, crushed
30ml olive oil
140g mange tout or sugar snaps
2 large courgettes, thinly sliced lengthways into ribbons using a vegetable peeler
100g chorizo or salami, sliced
4 individual goat's cheese rounds
4 fresh extra-large eggs, at room temperature
15ml white wine vinegar
sea salt and freshly ground black pepper

DRESSING
40ml balsamic vinegar
30ml olive oil
15ml whole-grain mustard
drizzle of honey

METHOD

Preheat the oven to 180°C and place the asparagus, red onion and garlic in a roasting pan. Drizzle with oil and season. Roast for 4 minutes, add the mange tout or sugar snaps and roast for 2 more minutes. Remove the asparagus and mange tout and leave the onion to cook for a further 10 minutes. Set aside.

Heat a griddle pan until hot. Brush the courgette slices with olive oil and griddle for 1-2 minutes on each side until charred. Arrange the vegetables on a serving platter together with the chorizo or salami slices and goat's cheese.

To poach the eggs, put enough water in a sauté pan to reach the ¾ mark. Bring to the boil and add the vinegar. Lower the heat and simmer gently. Crack the eggs into a measuring cup one at a time, then gently drop each one into the simmering water and cook for 3-4 minutes until the egg white has set but the yolk is still runny.

Remove the eggs with a slotted spoon and pat them with absorbent paper to lose the excess water before placing on the salad and seasoning.

For the dressing, mix all the ingredients together in a jug, drizzle over the salad and serve immediately.

Siba's tip...
The eggs must be fresh, otherwise poaching them will turn them into egg soup.

... *try something new* :-)

I HAVE CONSTANTLY TRIED NEW THINGS AND EXPERIMENTED IN THE KITCHEN, EVEN AS A CHILD, BECAUSE THAT'S HOW YOU LEARN. EVEN IF YOU FAIL, YOU LEARN.

...DON'T BE SHY!

STUFFED MUSHROOMS WITH QUAIL EGGS

THIS IS A GREAT MINI BREAKFAST WHEN YOU'RE LOOKING FOR A LITTLE TWIST TO THE CONTEMPORARY EGG BREAKFAST. I USUALLY SERVE IT WHEN I HAVE SEVERAL PEOPLE TO FEED AND AFTER A 'STARTER' OF EITHER PANCAKES, CEREALS OR COOKED PORRIDGE.

PREPARATION TIME: 10 MIN

COOKING TIME: 20 MIN

SERVES 6

6 very large brown
mushrooms, wiped
60ml melted butter
6 small thyme sprigs,
plus extra to garnish
1 onion, finely chopped
3 cloves garlic, crushed
1 red pepper, diced
1 green pepper, diced
salt and freshly ground
black pepper
12 spicy Italian salami slices
80ml Parmesan cheese,
grated (optional)
15ml oil
6 quail eggs

METHOD

Preheat the oven to 180°C and lightly grease a baking tray with oil. Remove the mushroom stems and arrange the caps on the prepared baking trays, stem side up. Generously brush each mushroom with butter, place a thyme sprig on each and bake for 5 minutes.

In the meantime, chop the stems and set aside. Heat the remaining butter and sauté the onion and garlic for 4 minutes until soft and slightly golden. Add the chopped mushroom stems and peppers, and cook for 3 minutes. Lightly season with salt and pepper and allow to cool slightly.

Remove the mushrooms from the oven and arrange two salami slices on each mushroom cap. Top the salami with the sautéed stuffing mixture and sprinkle with cheese. Bake for 5 minutes or until done.

Meanwhile, heat a non-stick frying pan until hot and brush with oil. Carefully crack each egg and cook for 2–3 minutes, or to your liking, and lightly season with sea salt. Remove the stuffed mushrooms from the oven and top each with a fried quail egg. Garnish with extra thyme and serve while warm.

Siba's tip...

The membranes of quail eggs are tougher than chicken eggs, so take care that the shells don't puncture the yolks while cracking them. As a variation to the fried egg topping, crack the eggs onto the stuffing mixture and bake in the oven with a sprinkle of grated cheese.

ANTIPASTI SALAD

This is one of my entertaining standards. It's so simple to make and uses a few fresh and good quality ingredients that just work well together. I usually use a variety of different-sized cherry tomatoes, some sliced and some on the vine.

PREPARATION TIME: 15 MIN
NO COOKING TIME
SERVES 4

350g red and yellow cherry
tomatoes, halved
250g tub bocconcini cheese
15ml fresh basil, torn
2 avocados, halved, stoned,
peeled and sliced
140g prosciutto slices
sea salt and freshly ground
black pepper, to taste

DRESSING
2 garlic cloves, crushed
30ml capers, finely chopped
60ml extra virgin olive oil
30ml balsamic vinegar
pinch of sugar

METHOD

Arrange the tomatoes and bocconcini on a large serving platter. Scatter the basil over them and add the avocado and prosciutto.

For the dressing, mix all the ingredients until the sugar has dissolved, then drizzle it over the salad. Serve with mini ciabatta breads or any lovely low GI bread of your choice.

Siba's tip...
To complement the capers in the dressing, you can also add a few sprigs of caperberries, which are the mature fruit of the caper bud, to your spread.

JUICY MEATBALL PITAS

PITAS ARE USUALLY OUR WEEKEND OR PICNIC THING, FOR THE OBVIOUS REASON THAT THEY'RE EASY TO MAKE, CONVENIENT TO PACK AND NO TROUBLE TO TRANSPORT IN A PICNIC BASKET. THEY ALSO MAKE A HANDY SCHOOL AND WORK LUNCH, BUT THE INGREDIENTS MUST BE PACKED SEPARATELY AND ASSEMBLED WHEN READY TO EAT OTHERWISE THE PITA BREAD WILL BECOME SOGGY.

PREPARATION TIME: 20 MIN
COOKING TIME: 25 MIN
SERVES 4

500g lean beef mince
2 onions, very finely chopped
2 cloves garlic, crushed
1 red pepper, grated
150ml fine dried breadcrumbs
30ml barbecue seasoning
30ml ground coriander
30ml ground cumin
handful fresh coriander, chopped
salt and pepper
30ml canola oil

SERVE WITH
4 pitas
30ml butter
60ml rocket
1 medium red onion, halved and
thinly sliced
125g cherry tomatoes, halved
tzatziki (see recipe on page 162)

METHOD

Place all the meatball ingredients together (except for the oil) in a large bowl and mix well to combine. Take one heaped tablespoon of the mixture and roll it in your hands to form a ball. Repeat with the rest of the mixture.

Heat the oil in a large non-stick frying pan. Add the meatballs and fry until golden brown on all sides. Cover the pan, reduce the heat to medium and cook for 5 minutes or so until cooked through.

To serve, spread the butter on either side of each pita. Heat a large non-stick frying pan and toast the pitas for about 2 minutes on each side until warm and puffed up. Cut in half and fill with rocket, red onion slices, tomatoes, meatballs and tzatziki.

Siba's tip...
If your frying pan does not have a lid to match, cover it with foil. To make the breadcrumbs, remove the crusts of 4 slices of brown bread and place them on a baking tray. Bake in a preheated oven at 200°C for 5 minutes. Allow to cool slightly and then blitz in a food processor to turn into crumbs.

SCAN TO WATCH
A VIDEO ON
HOW TO
MAKE THIS RECIPE

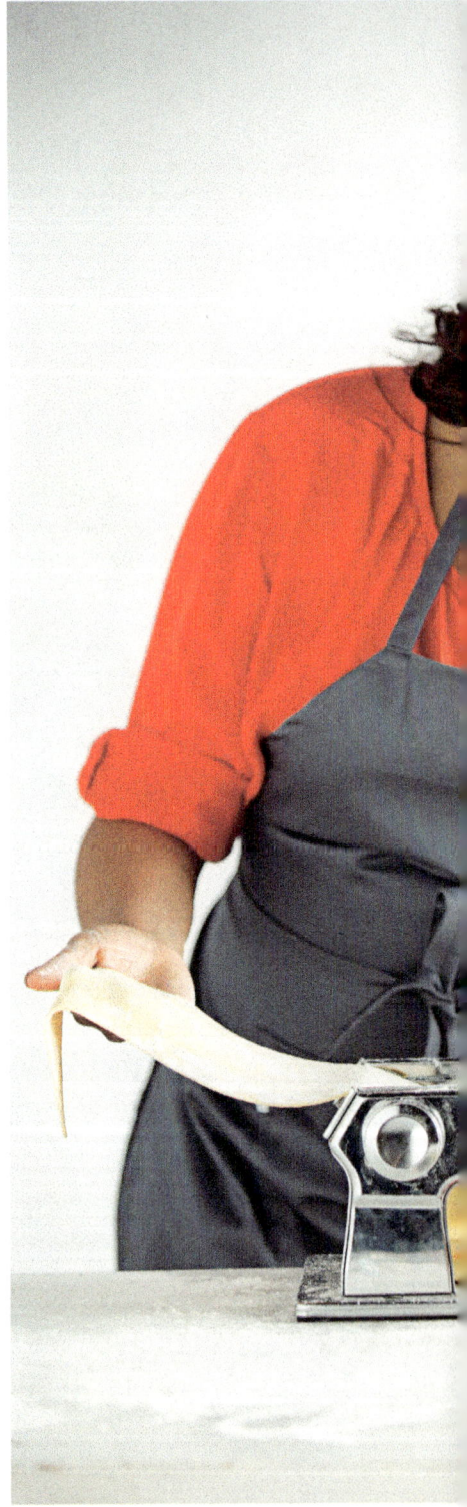

slowly, slowly —
no need to rush

make sure your parcels
have equal filling

CREAM CHEESE + SPINACH RAVIOLI

Making fresh pasta from scratch is a fulfilling experience and I really enjoy doing it, especially when I have free time to spend with my kitchen-loving and inquisitive son, Lonwabo. It's a bit of a labour of love, but the result is a world apart from dried pasta. All you need is a pasta machine and a bit of time. And, the pasta itself only requires three staple ingredients and water, that's it! Then it's the filling, which is uncomplicated.

METHOD

PREPARATION TIME: 40 MIN
CHILLING TIME: 15 MIN
COOKING TIME: 5 MIN
SERVES 4

500ml all-purpose flour
5ml salt
2 large eggs, beaten
60ml water

FILLING
250g tub cream cheese
500g spinach, thoroughly washed and wilted
salt and freshly ground black pepper, to taste
1 egg white,

BURNT BUTTER SAGE SAUCE
130ml salted butter
30ml fresh sage

SERVE WITH
75g pine nuts, toasted

Mix the flour and salt together in a bowl. Tip onto a clean working surface and make a hollow in the centre. Pour the beaten eggs into the hollow and mix using a fork or your hands until well combined. Add water, a little at a time, to form a pliable dough.

Knead the dough for 15–20 minutes. Chill in the fridge for at least 15 minutes. Now cut into 4 pieces and pass each one through the pasta machine starting with the thickest side (notch 1) first and moving to the thinner side until you have a long thin pasta sheet. Continue with the rest until you have four sheets.

Place one sheet on a floured surface, mix the cream cheese with the wilted spinach and season with salt and pepper. Drop spoonfuls of the mixture onto the sheet, leaving enough space between them to make individual ravioli.

Brush the whole sheet with egg white to glue the two sheets together. Place the second on top and press firmly with your index fingers to form a circular shape between and around each filling.

Now use a cookie cutter larger than the filling to cut through each one. Drop in salted boiling water and cook for 2–3 minutes until the pasta is al dente. Remove and gently pat dry.

For the sauce: heat the butter and sage until the butter has melted. Heat it for a further 2 minutes or so, watching it very closely, until it becomes a slightly dark golden brown colour with a nutty aroma. Serve the ravioli with a drizzle of the butter and a topping of toasted pinenuts.

CHICKEN PENNE PASTA

I FIRST MADE THIS DISH AS A PICNIC FOR A SIGHTSEEING TRIP AROUND CAPE TOWN WITH A VISITOR FROM KENYA, AND WE ENJOYED IT ON THE BEAUTIFUL CHAPMAN'S PEAK DRIVE WITH ITS BREATHTAKING VIEWS. IT HAS SINCE BECOME A STAND-BY MEAL FOR LAST-MINUTE DINNERS, LIKE WHEN BRIAN UNEXPECTEDLY BRINGS A FRIEND OR TWO HOME FROM WORK.

PREPARATION TIME: 10 MIN
COOKING TIME: 20 MIN
SERVES 3–4

500g penne, cooked al dente
salted water
45ml olive oil

PESTO CHICKEN
30ml oil from homemade pesto
(see recipe on page 157)
2 cloves garlic, crushed
4 chicken fillets, cut into strips
salt and freshly ground
black pepper
15ml dried Italian mixed herbs
250g cherry tomatoes, halved
60–90ml homemade pesto
juice and zest of 1 small lemon
Parmesan shavings, to garnish
fresh basil, to garnish

METHOD

Cook the penne in salted water and half the oil until al dente. Drain, drizzle with the remaining oil to prevent from sticking, and set aside.

Heat 15ml of the pesto oil in a large saucepan and sauté the garlic for a minute. Add the chicken strips and season with salt, pepper and dried Italian herbs. Sauté for 5 minutes until almost cooked through, and drizzle with the remaining oil to prevent sticking.

Add the cherry tomatoes and cook for a further 2 minutes. Combine with the cooked penne and enough basil pesto to coat the mix. Add a squeeze of lemon and the zest. Finish with Parmesan shavings and basil leaves, and serve warm or cold.

Siba's tip...
*My homemade pesto recipe has a naughty ingredient
– chili – which brightens and heats it up.*

GAZPACHO

I love the smell and feel of fresh ripe tomatoes. They remind me of my younger days, helping my mother pick them in her beautifully lush backyard garden. Then we'd wash and prep them for salads or tomato relishes and soups. This time I'm using them in an easy, uncooked, cold Spanish gazpacho soup which is my choice summer soup when I feel like something tasty and refreshing. I serve it in a glass alongside my canapés.

PREPARATION TIME: 10 MIN
NO COOKING TIME
SERVES 6

250g very ripe fresh tomatoes
1 clove garlic
½ celery stick, optional
5ml fresh basil, stems removed
plus extra to garnish
¼ small red onion, sliced
1 red pepper
30ml olive oil, plus extra
to drizzle
juice of a lemon wedge
60ml water
salt and pepper, to taste

SERVE WITH
10 ice blocks, crushed

METHOD

Place all the ingredients in a blender and whizz until smooth.

Pour into glasses and garnish with a drizzle of olive oil and basil. Pour the remainder into a jug with the crushed ice and garnish again with basil.

Siba's tip...

For your gazpacho to have a beautiful colour, it's important to use bright red and ripe tomatoes. To ripen tomatoes at home, place them in a perforated paper bag for a day or two. For a bit of spice, heat 15ml oil and sauté 5ml of smoked paprika for up to a minute and add it to the blended mixture. You can also roast the garlic clove in its peel in a preheated oven at 200°C for 10 minutes until it softens. Then remove the peel and continue with the recipe. This imparts less of a sharp garlic flavour.

NOT-SO-COLD 'GAZPACHO'

THIS IS ALMOST THE SAME GAZPACHO RECIPE AS THE ONE ON THE PREVIOUS PAGE. THE ONLY DIFFERENCE IS THAT IT'S MADE WITH LIGHTLY ROASTED RIPE TOMATOES, INSTEAD OF FRESH, TO GIVE IT A SLIGHTLY COOKED AND SWEETER FLAVOUR, AND IT'S OF COURSE WITHOUT THE CRUSHED ICE. I LOVE DIGGING MELBA TOAST INTO IT.

yum !!

DOUBLE CHEESE STRAWS

I NORMALLY USE THE ROLLED, FROZEN PUFF PASTRY THAT'S AVAILABLE IN SUPERMARKETS TO MAKE THESE. THEY'RE EASY TO RUSTLE UP AND SCRUMPTIOUS.

METHOD

PREPARATION TIME: 10 MIN
COOKING TIME: 15 MIN
MAKES 12

2 sheets ready rolled
puff pastry, thawed
30ml all-purpose flour,
to dust
30ml sweet chili sauce
125ml mozzarella, grated
125ml mature cheddar, grated
2ml chili flakes, to garnish
60ml sweet chili sauce,
to serve

Preheat the oven to 200°C and lightly grease a baking tray with butter.

Lay out one sheet of pastry on a lightly floured surface and spread the sweet chili sauce on top, using a brush or the back of a tablespoon.

Mix the grated cheeses together and sprinkle evenly over the pastry with sauce. Place the second pastry sheet on top and press down firmly. Cut into 12 long strips.

Pinch the ends of each strip firmly and twist on either side to create a spiral shape. Place on the prepared baking tray and bake for 15 minutes until puffed, golden and the cheese is melted.

Remove from the oven and stack on a board lined with parchment paper. Sprinkle with chili flakes and serve with sweet chili sauce for dipping.

Siba's tip...
When using frozen puff pastry, make sure you thaw it thoroughly in the fridge as it tends to crack and break otherwise. It's best to work with pastry on cooler days as heat can make it too soft, and difficult, to handle.

salads

& sides

Perfect for health-conscious working professionals on the go.

SAUTÉED GREENS WITH ROCKET + FETA

GROWING UP AT HOME, VEGETABLES FORMED AN IMPORTANT PART OF JUST ABOUT EVERY MEAL. I LOVED GOING INTO OUR VEGETABLE GARDEN WITH MY MOTHER TO HARVEST THE NECESSARY ITEMS FOR OUR MEALS AND HELPING HER TO WASH OFF THE SAND. THEN I WOULD WATCH HER CREATE MAGIC. ALTHOUGH I BUY MY VEGETABLES NOW, THEY'RE STILL A BIG FAVOURITE. I CONSTANTLY TRY OUT NEW CREATIVE COMBINATIONS. THIS RECIPE IS GREAT EITHER AS A SALAD OR A SIDE DISH.

PREPARATION TIME: 10 MIN
COOKING TIME: 10 MIN
SERVES 12

200g fine green beans, topped
200g broccolini stems
200g asparagus tips
200g snow peas
240g fresh peas
30ml olive oil
15ml butter
4 cloves garlic, finely chopped
10ml fresh ginger, peeled and grated
2ml crushed red chili flakes
salt and pepper, to taste

SERVE WITH
100–200g plain or herbed feta cheese
250g baby rocket, thoroughly washed

METHOD

Bring water to the boil in a large pot. Place a colander over it to create a steamer and steam the green vegetables for 3 minutes with the lid on. Remove and set aside.

In a large frying pan, heat the oil and butter, and sauté the garlic and ginger for a minute. Add the chili flakes and steamed vegetables, and cook for 2 minutes.

Then season with salt and pepper, transfer to a serving platter, and top with crumbled feta and rocket.

Siba's tip...
To shake things up a bit, I sometimes add roasted butternut and mixed bell peppers to this salad and substitute Gorgonzola cheese for the feta.

FRUIT CAMEMBERT SALAD

I ABSOLUTELY LOVE THIS SALAD AS IT'S A COMBINATION OF TWO THINGS I FIND HARD TO RESIST — CHEESE, ESPECIALLY CAMEMBERT, AND FRESH FRUITS. IT'S QUITE AN UNUSUAL COMBINATION, WHICH IS WHAT MAKES IT SPECIAL, AND IT SURE IS TASTY! TEN TO FIFTEEN MINUTES IS ALL YOU NEED TO MAKE IT.

PREPARATION: 10-15 MIN
NO COOKING TIME
SERVES 4

2 x 125g Camembert wheels
80g watercress, stems removed
250g strawberries, quartered and some sliced
75g raspberries
120g blueberries
4 oranges, peeled and cut into segments (optional)
3 kiwi fruits, peeled and sliced

DRESSING
75g strawberries
75g raspberries
juice of ½ orange
15ml balsamic reduction
15ml extra virgin olive oil, plus extra to drizzle
15ml Port wine

METHOD

On a big and beautiful platter, place the two cheeses on top of each other, slightly off the centre. Arrange the watercress, berries and fruit around it and place a few berries on top of the cheese.

For the dressing, blend the ingredients in a food processor until smooth. Pour it over the salad, and some on the side, just before serving. Drizzle with extra olive oil.

Siba's tip...
This salad also works well with fruit-flavoured cheeses. Try a sprinkle of freshly ground black pepper for a bit of punch.

BRAAIED CORN SALAD WITH BASIL PESTO

THIS SALAD TAKES ME BACK TO MY CHILDHOOD SUMMER HOLIDAYS WHEN BRAAING MEAT WAS THE NORM AND CORN WAS THE FLAGSHIP VEGETABLE. I HAVE SO MANY SALAD IDEAS TO BRING OUT THE FLAVOURS OF THIS COMBINATION, ESPECIALLY THE DISTINCT AND REFRESHING TASTE OF MINTY BASIL PESTO. IT'S ALWAYS A WINNER AT MY TABLE!

PREPARATION TIME: 10 MIN
COOKING TIME: 15 MIN
SERVES 8 AS A SIDE

6 corn cobs
60ml butter, melted
5ml garlic-and-herb seasoning,
to taste
2 cloves garlic, crushed
100g fine green beans,
halved lengthways
sea salt and freshly ground
black pepper
handful basil leaves, to garnish

PESTO DRESSING
250ml basil pesto
juice and zest of
½ lemon, to taste
2–3 fresh mint leaves,
finely chopped plus
extra to garnish

METHOD

Cook the corn in boiling, salted water for about 7 minutes or until tender. Drain, brush with half the butter, and season with the garlic-and-herb seasoning.

Place on the braai over hot coals or a hot griddle pan for 5 minutes until charred. Cut the corn kernels off the cobs and keep in a bowl.

Heat the remaining butter in a pan and sauté the garlic. Add the green beans, cook for 3 minutes and season with salt and pepper. Place the greens and the corn on a platter.

For the dressing, mix the pesto, zest and lemon juice with the finely chopped mint leaves. Drizzle over the salad just before serving, and scatter the basil and remaining mint leaves to garnish. It's great served warm or cold.

SCAN TO WATCH
A VIDEO ON
HOW TO
MAKE THIS RECIPE

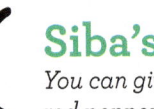

Siba's tip...
You can give this salad more substance by adding diced red pepper, spring onion and sliced mushrooms.

be sure to eat
your greens!

BACON WRAPPED GREENS

IT'S CURIOUS THAT CERTAIN DISHES I'VE CREATED ARE INSPIRED BY RANDOM INCIDENTS THAT HAVE NOTHING TO DO WITH FOOD. I CAME UP WITH THIS RECIPE AFTER SEEING A BEAUTIFUL GREEN AND BURNT ORANGE BRIDE BOUQUET THAT LOOKED EXQUISITE. IT INSPIRED THESE BUNDLES OF GREEN (VEGGIES) BOUND WITH BURNT ORANGE (BACON) 'RIBBON'. IT'S A GREAT HIT AT HOME AND GETS MY TWO OLDER BOYS (HUBBY BRIAN AND FIRST-BORN LONWABO) TO EAT THEIR VEGGIES, ESPECIALLY WHEN WRAPPED IN TWO RASHERS OF BACON!

PREPARATION TIME: 10 MIN
COOKING TIME: 5 MIN
SERVES UP TO 6

200g fine green beans
200g broccolini
200g asparagus
250g smoked bacon rashers
10ml olive oil
15ml brown sugar
15ml soy sauce

METHOD

Wrap 2 green beans, a long stem broccolini and an asparagus spear tightly in 1 or 2 smoked bacon rashers, and secure firmly with a toothpick.

Repeat until all the greens are tied together with the bacon rashers. Heat the oil in a large non-stick frying pan and place the bundles into it.

Lightly sprinkle them with brown sugar and a drizzle of soy sauce. Cook over high heat, turning until the bacon is cooked all round and golden in colour, and the veggies are still crispy.

Siba's tip...
Brown sugar, like all sugars, caramelises with heat and in this case it's used to brown and crispen the bacon quickly. Without it, the veggies would overcook while the bacon is browning. I love the umami flavour one gets from soy sauce, but its purpose here is to counteract the sweetness of the sugar without making the dish too salty.

BRAAIED BABY POTATOES + BACON

MY FRIENDS AND I OFTEN LAUGH ABOUT HOW IMPORTANT POTATOES WERE WHILE GROWING UP. A MEAL WASN'T COMPLETE WITHOUT THEM. WHETHER MASHED, BOILED AND SEASONED, FRIED OR AS A SALAD, THEY ALWAYS ACCOMPANIED OTHER VEGETABLES, SALADS, MEAT AND GRAVY. IT WAS THE SAME WITH BRAAING. THE FAMOUS POTATO SALAD ALWAYS FOUND ITS WAY ONTO THE MENU. THIS ALTERNATIVE TO THE TRUSTY POTATO SALAD IS A DELICIOUS COMBO WITH BACON THAT IS FINISHED OFF ON THE BRAAI.

PREPARATION TIME: 10 MIN
COOKING TIME: 35 MIN
SERVES 6-8

1kg baby new potatoes
salted water
45ml olive oil
250g smoked bacon rashers
15ml smoked paprika
10ml ground cumin
10ml ground coriander
coarse salt and freshly ground
black pepper, to taste
3 sprigs dill, chopped
15ml micro herbs, to garnish
(optional)

METHOD

In a large pan, par-boil the potatoes in salted boiling water for 10-15 minutes until just cooked. Drain the water, place back in the pan and put on a low heat for 3 minutes to steam dry.

In a little olive oil, fry the bacon until almost crispy. Add the spices and cook for a minute. Cut the potatoes in half and add them to the bacon and spices, tossing to coat them well. Add the remaining olive oil if the mix is too dry, and season with salt and pepper.

Remove from the heat and add the dill. Toss to combine. Take two large pieces of foil, tip the potato mix onto the centre of the two layers of foil and fold to create a parcel. Place the sealed parcel on the braai and cook for 15 minutes or so. Garnish with micro herbs, if using, just before serving.

SCAN TO WATCH
A VIDEO ON
HOW TO
MAKE THIS RECIPE

Siba's tip...
Make sure not to overcook the potatoes at the beginning as they'll become mushy and start breaking up when you toss them with the other ingredients.

PERFECT PICNIC PASTA

THIS SALAD CAME ABOUT WHEN I HAD AMPLE LEFTOVER INGREDIENTS FROM ANOTHER SALAD I HAD MADE WITH AVO, FETA, ROCKET, CUCUMBER AND CARROT RIBBONS TOPPED WITH A POACHED EGG AND A BALSAMIC DRESSING. NOT WANTING THE EXTRAS TO GO TO WASTE, I WHIZZED THEM ALL UP IN A FOOD PROCESSOR AND OUT CAME MY FIRST CREATION OF THIS CREAMY AVO DRESSING. IT'S A GREAT MATCH WITH PASTA AND HAS SINCE BEEN ADDED TO MY PICNIC RECIPE COLLECTION AS MY BOYS AND I LOVE IT. IT'S ALSO GREAT FOR AN AL FRESCO LUNCH AT HOME.

PREPARATION TIME: 15 MIN
COOKING TIME: 15 MIN
SERVES 4

200g farfalle (bow-tie) pasta
salted water
15ml olive oil, plus extra
to drizzle

CREAMY DRESSING
80g rocket
1 avocado
200g feta cheese
½ cucumber, cored and sliced
90ml basil pesto (see page 157
for recipe)
2ml salt
15ml fresh lemon juice
15ml balsamic vinegar

SERVE WITH
mixed cherry tomatoes,
some halved
mixed lettuce leaves
pine nuts, toasted

METHOD

Cook the pasta according to package instructions in salted water and a dash of oil until al dente.

Drain and, if the pasta is too sticky, rinse with warm water before draining some more. Drizzle with the extra olive oil and place aside to cool.

In a food processor, blend half the rocket and all the other creamy dressing ingredients until smooth. Gently mix with the pasta and tomatoes and the rest of the rocket.

Place the pasta onto a big platter or picnic dish with the lettuce leaves. Top with pine nuts for a crunch and a beautiful garnish. Cover if going on a picnic or serve as is at home.

Siba's tip...
You could replace the nuts with a mix of toasted seeds, such as flax, sunflower and butternut. If you're not fond of avocado, then use 80ml cream cheese instead, bearing in mind that the colour won't be as green.

SALADS + SIDES

=59

PUTTANESCA SALAD

I LOVE THE FLAVOURS OF PUTTANESCA SAUCE, WHICH IS TRADITIONALLY SERVED WITH PASTA AND SOMETIMES CRUSTY BREAD FOR MOPPING UP LEFTOVER SAUCE. I THINK IT'S THE DISTINCTNESS OF THE ANCHOVY THAT REMINDS ME OF THE ANCHOVY PASTE I ENJOYED ON MY SANDWICHES GROWING UP. SINCE THEN, I'VE WANTED A CARB-LIGHT VERSION OF THE PASTA DISH (HENCE THIS SALAD) THAT I CAN ENJOY AT MIDDAY WITHOUT FEELING TOO FULL. THE MARINATED ARTICHOKE HEARTS ARE A 'SIBALICIOUS' ADDITION TO THE USUAL PUTTANESCA FLAVOURS AND THEY COMPLEMENT THE OTHER INGREDIENTS VERY WELL.

PREPARATION TIME: 10 MIN
NO COOKING TIME
SERVES 3

40g wild rocket
250g cherry tomatoes, some
halved and some whole
1 red onion, thinly sliced
1 red pepper, cut into strips
10ml caperberries,
finely chopped
12 pitted Kalamata olives
4 anchovies, finely chopped
3 marinated artichoke hearts,
roughly chopped
1 large handful basil leaves,
roughly torn

DRESSING
4 anchovies, finely chopped
80ml olive oil
15ml red wine vinegar
juice and zest of ½ lemon
honey or sugar, to taste
(optional)

METHOD

On a serving platter arrange all the salad ingredients in layers, finishing with the fresh basil. Toss well.

Mix the dressing ingredients in a jar or jug and mix or shake until well combined. Drizzle over the salad just before serving.

Siba's tip...
You can use either capers or caperberries. Make sure the anchovies are finely chopped – a big piece can be too much for one bite.

GRILLED CORN SALAD

IT'S HARD TO BELIEVE THAT CORN ORIGINATED IN MEXICO AND NOT IN AFRICA AS IT'S SUCH A STAPLE OF THE AFRICAN DIET. WE EAT BRAAIED, STEAMED OR BOILED CORN ON THE COB, MAIZE MEAL IN A VARIETY OF GUISES AND, OF COURSE, THE SAMP AND BEANS I GREW UP WITH. THIS RECIPE IS A CELEBRATION, AND REMINDER, OF THE ORIGIN OF CORN, HENCE THE MEXICAN FLAVOURS OF LIME, CILANTRO (ALSO KNOWN AS CORIANDER OR DHANIA) AND TEQUILA IN THE DRESSING, WHICH GIVE THIS OTHERWISE SIMPLE SALAD A WONDERFUL KICK.

PREPARATION TIME: 10 MIN
COOKING TIME: 20 MIN
SERVES 6

6 small corn cobs
sea salt and freshly ground black pepper, to taste
180g very fine green beans, tailed
30ml olive oil
1 avocado, peeled and sliced
30ml coriander, torn

DRESSING
30ml lime juice
30ml honey
10ml tequila
1 clove garlic, crushed
60ml extra virgin olive oil
5ml coriander, chopped
(optional)

METHOD

Soak the cobs in hot water for 10 minutes or boil for 5 minutes until just tender. Remove them from the water and season with salt and pepper. Braai on an open fire or a griddle pan over the stove for about 10 minutes, turning often until they're charred.

Place the beans in a bowl. Drizzle over some olive oil, season with salt and pepper, and toss. Put them in a grill basket, or directly on a griddle pan, and grill for 5-7 minutes, turning them so they cook evenly. Allow the beans and cobs to cool.

Cut the corn kernels off 3 of the cobs and halve or slice the rest before putting them on a platter. Add the beans and avo to the salad, sprinkle with the coriander and toss lightly. For the dressing, place all the ingredients in a jar or jug and shake or stir until well combined. Drizzle with the dressing just before serving.

SCAN TO WATCH
A VIDEO ON
HOW TO
MAKE THIS RECIPE

Siba's tip...
When braaing, make sure the grill is clean and brushed with oil to prevent the cobs from sticking to it. If you're not braaing the cobs, cook them on the stove in a griddle pan over high heat to get the charring. If you have a gas stove, you can cook the cobs directly on the gas heat for charring and a smoky flavour.

BEET + GOAT'S CHEESE WITH A CITRUS DRESSING

This is one of my many trusted starter recipes. The sweet and earthy flavour of the raw beet balances well with the citrus dressing, and I like to make this when I'm feeding a large number of people, either at home or when catering for a special function. It's an easy-to-make crowd pleaser that combines fresh, creamy, tangy and some crunch in one delicious starter.

PREPARATION TIME: 10 MIN
NO COOKING TIME
SERVES 6-8

6 beetroots, thoroughly washed
2 x 140g goat's cheese logs
100g pistachio nuts, finely chopped
100g watercress, stems removed
2 sticks of celery, cut in slices lengthways
handful of celery leaves, to garnish

CITRUS DRESSING
30ml naartjie, mandarin or tangerine juice
30ml lemon juice
5ml whole-grain mustard
30ml olive oil
honey, to taste

METHOD

Slice the raw beetroot thinly using a mandolin. Cut the goat's cheese logs into thick slices, shape them into rounds and roll them in the chopped pistachio nuts.

Arrange the watercress and beetroot, celery and goat's cheese slices on a platter. Mix the citrus dressing and drizzle it over the salad before garnishing with the celery leaves.

Siba's tip...
If you'd prefer to cook the beetroots, place them in a large pan, cover with cold water and a lid, and cook for about 20 minutes. Rinse with cold water to cool them enough to handle, peel off the skin – using gloves or with hands rubbed in oil to avoid them turning purple – then thinly slice and chill.

GINGER + CORIANDER CORN SALAD

WHENEVER I MEET FANS ON THE STREET, IN MALLS OR VIA SOCIAL MEDIA, THIS IS A RECIPE THAT IS OFTEN COMMENTED ON. I REFER TO IT AS THE 'RAINBOW NATION CORN SALAD' ON SIBA'S TABLE COOKING SHOW BECAUSE IT'S SO COLOURFUL AND FULL OF DIFFERENT FLAVOURS. IT'S BEAUTIFUL TOO.

PREPARATION TIME: 10 MIN
COOKING TIME: 15 MIN
SERVES 8

15ml olive oil
250g smoked streaky bacon, chopped
1 onion, finely chopped
4 cloves garlic, finely chopped
30ml fresh ginger, finely grated
1 red pepper, diced
1 green pepper, diced
1 yellow pepper, diced
250g button mushrooms, thinly sliced
750g frozen corn, defrosted in a sieve under warm running water
30ml fresh coriander, chopped
60ml Kikkoman's soy sauce
pinch of freshly ground black pepper

METHOD

Heat the oil in a large frying pan and fry the bacon and onion for about 5 minutes until the bacon is slightly crispy and the onions are soft and golden. Add the garlic and half of the ginger and cook for another minute.

Add the peppers and mushrooms and cook for 4 minutes until the mushrooms are soft and the peppers slightly soft. Add the corn and coriander and stir to combine, followed by the soy sauce, black pepper and remaining ginger.

Serve immediately, while warm.

SCAN TO WATCH
A VIDEO ON
HOW TO
MAKE THIS RECIPE

Siba's tip...

When preparing mushrooms, it's best to wipe them with a clean tea towel rather than wash or rinse them as they soak up water (like sponges) which then oozes out while sautéing. Make sure you don't overcook the veggies.

JARRED SALAD

I OFTEN MAKE JARRED SALADS FOR PICNICS AS THEY'RE EASY TO CARRY IN A BASKET. I LOVE THIS FRESH HERBED RASPBERRY DRESSING AS IT COMPLEMENTS THE SALAD WELL. I TEND TO MAKE LARGE BATCHES OF IT AND CHILL IT IN AN AIRTIGHT CONTAINER IN THE FRIDGE FOR TWO DAYS AT THE MOST.

METHOD

PREPARATION TIME: 15–20 MIN
NO COOKING TIME
SERVES 3

1 cucumber, cut into
ribbons or sticks
3 baby purple carrots,
halved lengthwise
½ red onion, thinly sliced
100g green olives, pitted
100g Kalamata olives, pitted
250g feta cheese
basil leaves, to garnish

DRESSING
60ml red wine vinegar
45ml olive oil
5ml fresh oregano, chopped
5ml fresh basil, chopped
2ml fresh thyme, chopped
2ml garlic flakes
2ml onion powder
2ml Dijon mustard
2ml whole-grain mustard
45ml raspberries
pinch of salt and freshly ground
black pepper and sugar, to taste

Place equal numbers of cucumber ribbons or sticks and carrots in three jars, followed by the red onion, olives and feta cheese.

For the dressing, blend all the dressing ingredients together until smooth, and place in a separate jar with a lid.

Close and chill the salad and dressing jars until serving time. Then garnish the salad with basil leaves and drizzle it with dressing just before serving.

Siba's tip...
Don't overfill the jar as there needs to be enough space to drizzle the dressing.

ASIAN RIBBON SALAD

THIS IS A POW-WOW SALAD USING SIMPLE INGREDIENTS, THOUGH THE EDAMAME BEANS ADD A CERTAIN SOPHISTICATION AND THE DRESSING PACKS A PUNCH. I USUALLY SERVE IT WITH MY ASIAN-INSPIRED SURF AND TURF MEAL OF ROASTED BEEF FILLET AND CALAMARI WITH SUSHI RICE. IT HAS LOTS OF VEGETABLES IN IT, SO YOU NEED NOTHING EXTRA. AND IT'S GREAT AS A SALAD ON ITS OWN TOO.

METHOD

PREPARATION TIME: 15 MIN
COOKING TIME: 5 MIN
SERVES 6

100g edamame beans
2 large carrots, sliced
into ribbons
1 large cucumber, sliced into
thin ribbons
2 pimentos, thinly sliced
lengthways
100g baby corn, sliced
50ml bean sprouts
50ml coriander

DRESSING
25ml soy sauce
15ml sesame oil
25ml rice wine vinegar
1 long spring onion,
finely chopped
7ml fresh ginger, grated
30ml coriander, finely chopped
1 clove garlic, crushed
80ml coconut cream
2ml (7 drops) Tabasco sauce
pinch of sugar, to taste

Bring a large saucepan half-filled with water, to the boil. Place a colander over the pot to create a steamer and place the edamame beans inside. Cover with a lid and steam for 5 minutes. Set aside to cool slightly, then remove the beans from their shells.

Layer the salad ingredients on a platter. Toss slightly. Mix the dressing ingredients in a jar or jug and shake or stir well. Drizzle over the salad just before serving.

Siba's tip...
Since this salad is so easy to make, the vegetables can be prepared beforehand, while the dressing can be made in advance. Use a vegetable peeler to slice the vegetables into ribbons.

SALADS + SIDES

I TEND TO THIN

IS LIKE COMPOSING MUSIC.

CONTRIBUTE TO THE WHOLE

REST. TOGETHER, ALL THE

A GLORIOUS MELODY ——

IT SHOULD MAKE PERFECT

TO FIND THEMSELVES TOGET

K THAT MAKING A SALAD

EVERY INGREDIENT SHOULD

AND NEVER OVERPOWER THE

NOTES COMBINE TO CREATE

NEVER HARSH OR GRATING.

SENSE FOR THE INGREDIENTS

HER IN ONE BOWL."

HERBY POTATO SALAD

THIS IS A PERSONAL TAKE ON THE TRADITIONAL POTATO SALAD. INSTEAD OF MAYO I USE CRÈME FRAÎCHE WITH HERBS AS A DRESSING, WHICH JAZZES IT UP A BIT, AND I SOMETIMES CRUSH THE POTATOES SLIGHTLY WITH THE SKIN ON OR KEEP THEM WHOLE.

PREPARATION TIME: 5 MIN
COOKING TIME: 15 MIN
SERVES 6

300g red baby potatoes
15ml crème fraîche
20ml fresh parsley, chopped
20ml fresh dill, chopped, plus extra to garnish
salt and freshly ground black pepper
30ml olive oil
pink peppercorns, to garnish

METHOD

Place the potatoes in a saucepan and cover with cold salted water. Bring to the boil and cook for about 10–15 minutes until the potatoes are tender. Drain, place on a low heat to remove the excess water, then cool the potatoes very slightly, before halving or crushing them.

Add the crème fraîche and herbs and stir. Place on a serving plate as a side dish. Season well with salt and pepper. Drizzle with olive oil and finish with extra dill and the pink peppercorns.

SCAN TO WATCH
A VIDEO ON
HOW TO
MAKE THIS RECIPE

Siba's tip...

This recipe goes very well with the stuffed + baked salmon on page 134. I first prepared it for a romantic dinner for two with Brian when Lonwabo was still a baby and would only allow a date night in – it was an instant hit!

RED BEAN SALAD

I ALWAYS HAVE A FEW TINS OF BEANS IN MY PANTRY BECAUSE THEY'RE SO VERSATILE. IN THIS RECIPE, I PAIR THEM WITH FRESH AND CRISPY RADISHES, SWEET AND SOUR PEPPADEWS, A SWEET AND CRISPY RED ONION AND A PUNCHY DRESSING. TOGETHER IT ALL TASTES HEAVENLY. SINCE THERE'S NO COOKING INVOLVED I JUST MIX EVERYTHING UP, RELAX AND TUCK IN AT MY LEISURE.

PREPARATION TIME: 10 MIN
NO COOKING TIME
SERVES 6

400g can red kidney beans, drained and rinsed
8 radishes, sliced
1 red onion, thinly sliced
5 Peppadews, sliced

DRESSING
60ml sour cream
60ml mayonnaise
60ml buttermilk or sour milk
juice of ¼ lime
1 clove garlic, crushed
30ml fresh coriander, chopped
sea salt and freshly ground
black pepper, to taste
2ml sugar, to taste
35ml micro herbs, to garnish

METHOD

Mix the salad ingredients together in a large bowl and toss well. Then combine the dressing ingredients, and season with salt, pepper and sugar to taste.

Arrange the salad on a serving platter and drizzle over the dressing. Garnish with micro herbs to serve.

SCAN TO WATCH
A VIDEO ON
HOW TO
MAKE THIS RECIPE

Siba's tip...
I like making a few crostini and scooping the salad onto them for a bit of a change.

HERBY COUSCOUS, BUTTERNUT + FETA SÁLAD

THIS IS MY QUICK AND EASY 'CHEAT' BUTTERNUT AND COUSCOUS SALAD. ORIGINALLY, I CREATED THIS SALAD USING ROASTED BUTTERNUT BUT AS YOU MAY KNOW, ROASTING BUTTERNUT TAKES UP TO 45 MINUTES IN THE OVEN. SO, WHEN I'M IN A BIG HURRY, I BUY BUTTERNUT IN A MICROWAVE-SAFE BAG AND MICROWAVE IT FOR 5 MINUTES UNTIL COOKED AND TENDER. I THEN HEAT A LARGE NON-STICK FRYING PAN AND SAUTÉ THE BUTTERNUT IN BUTTER FOR 5 MINUTES UNTIL IT'S GOLDEN BROWN AND LOOKS LIKE IT HAS BEEN ROASTED. IT SAVES MORE THAN 30 MINUTES OF COOKING TIME!

PREPARATION TIME: 15 MIN
COOKING TIME: 10 MIN
SERVES 4

400g (1 pack) cubed butternut, store-bought
500ml couscous
pinch of salt
30ml butter

VINAIGRETTE
15ml Dijon mustard
80ml olive oil
juice of 1 lemon
30ml fresh Italian parsley, chopped
30ml fresh mint, chopped
30ml fresh chives, chopped
pinches of salt and pepper, to taste

GARNISH
60g wild rocket, washed
10ml mint
30ml honey, to taste
75g feta cheese, crumbled
60ml pomegranate rubies

METHOD

Microwave the butternut cubes in their microwave-safe bag for 5 minutes, until tender. Place the couscous in a large, deep dish and cover with sufficient boiling water to end up with about a centimetre of water above the surface of the couscous. Stir in a pinch of salt.

Cover the dish with plastic wrap and leave it for about 10 minutes, until the granules have swelled up and doubled in size, and the water has been absorbed.

Heat the butter in a large frying pan and sauté the cooked butternut for about 5 minutes until it's golden brown all over.

Place the vinaigrette ingredients into a mini food processor and whizz until fine, or finely chop the herbs and mix everything together in a small bowl.

Fluff the couscous with a fork. Add the 'roasted' butternut, wild rocket, vinaigrette and honey, and toss. Tip onto a serving platter, sprinkle over the feta and garnish with the pomegranate rubies and some extra fresh herbs.

Siba's tip...
If you prefer to roast the butternut, place the cubes on a greased baking tray, dot with butter and drizzle with honey. Roast in an oven preheated to 180°C for 40–45 minutes until lightly golden. You might have to turn them once.

RED KIDNEY BEAN + AVO SALAD

WITH MY BUSY WORK SCHEDULE, I SOMETIMES DON'T HAVE ENOUGH TIME TO DO THE WEEKLY GROCERY SHOPPING, BUT THAT'S HOW THIS RECIPE CAME ABOUT. I HAD ONLY A FEW INGREDIENTS LEFT IN MY PANTRY AND, WHEN I PUT THEM TOGETHER, THIS SALAD EMERGED. BRIAN LOVES IT, SO NOW WE OFTEN HAVE IT AS A SIDE DISH FOR LUNCH OR SUPPER.

PREPARATION TIME: 10 MIN
NO COOKING TIME
SERVES 6

2 bags of mixed salad leaves
400g can red kidney beans, drained and rinsed
150g black pepper feta cheese, crumbled
3 firm and ripe avocados, sliced
½ cucumber, sliced into long thin ribbons using a vegetable peeler
½ lemon

DRESSING
125ml balsamic vinegar
15ml honey
80ml extra virgin olive oil
salt and freshly ground black pepper, to taste

METHOD

Pour the salad leaves onto a large platter. Top with the kidney beans, feta and avocado. Fold the ribbons of cucumber into concertina shapes and tuck them in amongst the other salad ingredients.

Squeeze the lemon juice over the avo to prevent it from turning brown. Mix the dressing ingredients together and drizzle over the salad just before serving.

SCAN TO WATCH
A VIDEO ON
HOW TO
MAKE THIS RECIPE

Siba's tip...
Make sure the salad leaves are rinsed and ready to eat. If they aren't, rinse them thoroughly and pat dry with kitchen roll before using.

BEET + FETA SALAD

The flavour profile of this recipe is very similar to the onion-and-pickled beet dish that I grew up eating. This is just a little glammed up. It's also an uncomplicated dish that can serve both as an accompaniment and a meal on its own.

PREPARATION TIME: 10 MIN
COOKING TIME: 20 MIN
SERVES 8

8 medium beetroots, washed with stems removed
1 red onion, sliced
150g feta cheese, roughly crumbled
50g pine or pistachio nuts, toasted
2 baby spring onions, finely sliced
30ml crimson micro herbs, to garnish

DRESSING
80ml mayonnaise
80ml chutney
20ml balsamic vinegar

METHOD

Cook the beetroots in water for 15–20 minutes. Remove from the heat and rinse under cold running water. Rub your hands with oil or wear gloves to avoid staining your skin, and peel off the beet skins before leaving to cool completely.

Halve or quarter the beetroots and mix them with the red onion. Place on a platter and top with the feta cheese, roasted nuts, spring onions and crimson micro herbs. Or, alternatively, chill in the fridge until needed.

Combine the dressing ingredients and pour over the salad before serving.

SALADS + SIDES

SCAN TO WATCH
A VIDEO ON
HOW TO
MAKE THIS RECIPE

Siba's tip...
You can also half-cook the beets for extra texture.

BAKED CHICKEN STRIPS

THESE ARE LONWABO'S FAVOURITE, ESPECIALLY WHEN DIPPED IN KETCHUP OR ANY OTHER DIPPING SAUCE. THEY'RE ALSO GREAT FOR PICNICS AND FOR LUNCH, AS LONG AS THEY'VE COOLED DOWN BEFORE BEING PACKED INTO A CLOSED TUB. I LIKE THE FACT THAT THEY'RE BAKED, NOT FRIED, ESPECIALLY AS A KIDDY SNACK.

PREPARATION TIME: 10 MIN
COOKING TIME: 7 MIN
SERVES 3-4

180ml dried breadcrumbs
45ml Parmesan cheese, finely grated
15ml dried oregano
7ml garlic flakes
5ml onion powder
15ml chicken stock powder
2ml salt
2ml freshly ground black pepper
2 medium eggs
3 chicken fillets
5ml butter, melted

SERVE WITH
200g mixed leaves
4 radishes, sliced

METHOD

Preheat the oven to 180°C and lightly grease a baking tray with cooking spray. Mix the breadcrumbs with the cheese, oregano, garlic flakes, onion and chicken stock powders, salt and pepper, and transfer to a flat plate.

Whisk the eggs and place them next to the breadcrumb mix. Cut the chicken fillets into strips. Coat each strip in crumbs, dip them in egg and coat them in crumbs again. Continue until all the strips are coated. Place the strips individually on the prepared tray and dab with melted butter using a brush.

Bake the strips for 5 minutes, then turn and bake them for 2 more minutes to crispen the other sides. They can be served warm or cold on a bed of mixed leaves and radishes, or just as they are, along with a dipping sauce.

Siba's tip...
If you don't have garlic flakes and onion powder, add 2 cloves of crushed garlic and a small wedge of very finely grated onion to the egg before beating it.

ITALIAN SALAD

THIS IS AN IDEAL SALAD FOR SHOWING OFF GOOD-QUALITY FRESH TOMATOES, AND A GREAT SIDE DISH FOR SUMMER. YOU CAN GLAM IT UP BY ADDING BALLS OF CREAMY MOZZARELLA.

PREPARATION TIME: 10 MIN
NO COOKING TIME
SERVES 4

350g mixed tomatoes in different colours and sizes, some sliced, some quartered and some smaller ones left whole
50g green olives
50g Kalamata olives, halved
10ml capers
15ml fresh basil, chopped
30ml garlic-flavoured extra virgin olive oil
pinch of sea salt and freshly ground black pepper
small bunch whole basil leaves

METHOD

Prepare the tomatoes and place on a platter. Add the olives, capers, and chopped basil.

Drizzle over the garlic-flavoured olive oil. Season with salt and pepper, and garnish with a small bunch of whole basil leaves.

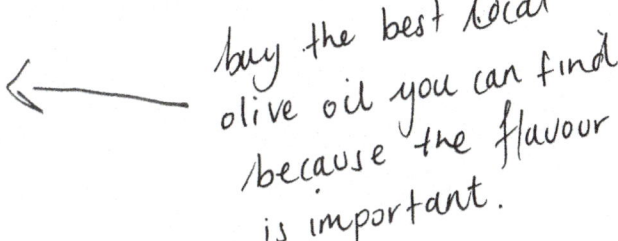

buy the best local olive oil you can find because the flavour is important.

SCAN TO WATCH
A VIDEO ON
HOW TO
MAKE THIS RECIPE

Siba's tip...

Try to get the very best tomatoes, preferably from an early morning organic market. Pick the juiciest, plumpest tomatoes you can find – heavy and dense, as if ready to burst. And make sure they're completely ripe, with no greenness around the stem. The same goes for the olive oil – buy the best because the flavour is important.

MARINATED CUCUMBERS WITH BLACK SESAME SEEDS

THIS IS A SIMPLE SIDE DISH THAT I OFTEN SERVE WITH AN ASIAN-INSPIRED MEAL. IT'S SO EASY TO MAKE AND I LOVE THE CITRUS FLAVOURS OF THE MARINADE AS THEY GIVE IT A SUBTLE PICKLED TASTE.

PREPARATION TIME: 5 MIN
MARINATING TIME: 10-15 MIN
NO COOKING TIME
SERVES 4

1 large cucumber, cut into spears

MARINADE
90ml rice vinegar
5ml soy sauce
juice of ½ naartjie, mandarin or tangerine
30ml sugar

GARNISH
5ml black sesame seeds
Italian parsley
1 purple spring onion, finely cut into strips

METHOD

Place the cucumber spears on a shallow serving dish.

Mix the marinade ingredients together, pour it over the cucumber, then cover and leave to marinate for at least 15 minutes in the fridge. Sprinkle with the black sesame seeds, Italian parsley and spring onion strips before serving.

SCAN TO WATCH
A VIDEO ON
HOW TO
MAKE THIS RECIPE

HARISSA TABBOULEH

I love this Middle Eastern dish made with bulgur wheat. When I visited Dubai, I noticed there were different grades of bulgur wheat and each was defined by how finely mealed it was. In South Africa, the common one is the more granular variation and I thought I'd bring it home with a touch of the North African, and fiery, harissa paste.

PREPARATION TIME: 15 MIN
COOKING TIME: 10 MIN
SERVES 4-6

500ml salted water
250ml uncooked bulgur wheat

DRESSING
5ml homemade harissa paste
(see recipe on page 172)
30ml extra virgin olive oil
juice of ½ lemon
5ml sugar or honey
pinch of sea salt and freshly ground
black pepper, to taste

SALAD
400g cherry tomatoes, halved
1 red onion, thinly sliced
4 spring onions including the
green part, chopped
1 red pepper, diced
½ cucumber, cored and sliced
60ml Italian parsley, chopped
30ml fresh mint, chopped, plus
extra to garnish
5ml dried spearmint
50g flaked and toasted almonds,
to garnish
pomegranate rubies, to garnish

METHOD

Bring the salted water to the boil. Add the bulgur wheat, bring to the boil again, then cover and simmer for 10 minutes or until the water has evaporated completely and the bulgur wheat is cooked. Cool slightly.

Mix the dressing ingredients together and whisk well until combined, then set aside. Combine the salad ingredients with the cooked and cooled bulgur wheat.

Tip onto a large serving platter and serve with the dressing. Top with the toasted almonds to garnish.

SCAN TO WATCH
A VIDEO ON
HOW TO
MAKE THIS RECIPE

Siba's tip...
With its minty flavour, this salad is also great on a mezze platter. You can also add a few pomegranate rubies to the garnish.

ASIAN SLAW

I GREW UP WITH COLESLAW. WE HAD IT WEEKLY, ON SUNDAYS, AND IT WAS ALWAYS SERVED AT GATHERINGS AND ON SPECIAL OCCASIONS. SO, BY THE TIME I REACHED ADULTHOOD IT HAD BECOME OLD HAT. I THEN DECIDED TO GIVE IT A NEW LEASE ON LIFE BY INFUSING THE MAYO WITH GINGER, WASABI AND SOY. WHILE THESE FLAVOURS ARE NORMALLY ASSOCIATED WITH SUSHI, THEY'RE ALSO FABULOUS WITH SLAW.

PREPARATION TIME: 5 MIN
NO COOKING TIME
SERVES 6

200g (¼ of a medium) white cabbage, shredded
200g (¼ of a medium) red cabbage, shredded
220g (2 large) carrots, washed and shredded
2 spring onions, chopped diagonally
3ml fresh coriander, finely chopped, plus extra to garnish
100g bean sprouts

DRESSING
400ml mayonnaise
7ml wasabi paste
3ml fresh or pickled ginger, grated
10ml soy sauce
30ml water
2ml red peppercorns (optional)

METHOD

Place the shredded cabbages, carrots, spring onions, coriander and bean sprouts in a bowl and mix together.

Combine the dressing ingredients in a jar or jug and pour over the salad, mixing it in thoroughly. Transfer to a serving bowl and garnish with a few coriander leaves.

SALADS + SIDES

SCAN TO WATCH
A VIDEO ON
HOW TO
MAKE THIS RECIPE

Siba's tip...
It's far quicker and less of a mess to shred the cabbages and carrots using the shredding attachment of a food processor. Unlike with most salads, it's better to add the dressing to a slaw way before serving time.

ME

MEAT & poultry

I'd never last as a vegetarian – I just love meat and chicken.

ROAST LAMB WITH GRAVY

Lamb roast is a favourite for Sundays and special occasions. I make deep incisions all around the lamb and stuff them with rosemary, thyme and garlic slices, thus allowing the flavour to penetrate deep into the meat. I then cover the entire surface with a wet rub for extra taste and slow roast it. The result always pleases everyone, and it's just delicious with the mint and mustard gravy.

PREPARATION TIME: 20 MIN
COOKING TIME: 4½ HRS
SERVES 8

2.7kg leg of lamb
5 cloves garlic, roughly sliced
30ml fresh thyme
30ml fresh rosemary
250ml low-sodium chicken stock
100ml water

WET RUB

15 fresh mint leaves, chopped
4 cloves garlic, crushed
60ml olive oil
60ml mayonnaise
10ml whole-grain mustard
2ml English mustard powder
juice and zest of 1 lemon
freshly ground black pepper

MINT + MUSTARD GRAVY

5ml whole-grain mustard
6 torn mint leaves
30ml crème fraîche
2ml honey, to taste
125ml chicken stock

METHOD

Preheat the oven to 140°C. Place the lamb on a surface and make deep but small incisions all over the meat with a sharp knife. Stuff each incision with sliced garlic, thyme and rosemary sprigs.

For the wet rub, mix together the mint, crushed garlic, olive oil, mayonnaise, whole grain mustard, mustard powder, lemon juice and zest in a small bowl. Rub it all over the lamb.

Place the remaining fresh thyme and rosemary in the roasting tin, and place the leg of lamb on top. Pour the stock and water into the roasting tin around the meat, and cover with tin foil to seal.

Roast in the oven at 140°C for 4 hours or until very tender. Increase the temperature to 180°C, remove the tin foil, return and roast for 30 minutes until golden. Remove from the oven and transfer the lamb to a serving board, to rest while you make the gravy.

For the gravy, take the roasting tin and spoon off the excess fat, then place it on the hob and bring to a rapid boil. Add the mustard, mint leaves, crème fraîche, and some honey for taste. Pour in the stock and bring to the boil. Season, pass through a sieve into a gravy boat, and serve with the meat.

Siba's tip...

A perfectly slow-roasted lamb needs to be tender and fall off the bone. So make sure to check that yours is cooked properly before removing the foil and browning it. If there's any leftover meat, you can make gourmet sandwiches with it, such as lamb with roasted butternut or beet, rocket and feta. You can also add the shredded lamb strips to a vegetable stir fry just a few minutes before the vegetables are done.

SCAN TO WATCH
A VIDEO ON
HOW TO
MAKE THIS RECIPE

MEAT + POULTRY

STICKY CHICKEN WINGS

THESE ALWAYS COME IN HANDY WHEN I HAVE A LARGE GROUP OF PEOPLE COMING OVER AND WANT A CASUAL, TAPAS-STYLE MENU.
MY GIRLFRIENDS LOVE THEM AND SO DO MY BOYS AT HOME, WHO NEVER SEEM TO GET ENOUGH OF THEM! THEY'RE SO FLAVOURSOME
AND DELICIOUS WHO CAN RESIST THESE LITTLE TREATS?

PREPARATION TIME: 5 MIN
COOKING TIME: 20 MIN
SERVES 5

20 chicken wings
2 cloves garlic, crushed
30ml fresh ginger, grated
sea salt and freshly ground
black pepper

MARINADE
60ml soy sauce
250ml sweet chili sauce
250ml smoky barbecue sauce

SERVE WITH
15ml micro coriander
4 spring onions, finely sliced
lengthways
10ml white sesame seeds
2 limes, wedged (optional)

METHOD

Preheat the oven to 200°C and lightly grease a roasting tray with oil or cooking spray. In a large bowl, rub the crushed garlic and ginger into the chicken wings and season well with salt and pepper.

Combine the marinade ingredients in a jug and pour over the wings, mixing until fully coated. Transfer to the prepared roasting tray, making sure that the wings don't overlap.

Roast for 15–20 minutes, until the wings are cooked through and golden. Transfer to a large serving platter and garnish with the micro coriander, spring onions, sesame seeds and the optional squeeze of lime.

MEAT + POULTRY

SCAN TO WATCH
A VIDEO ON
HOW TO
MAKE THIS RECIPE

Siba's tip...

To get the finest flavour, it's best to marinate the wings for at least 30 minutes in the fridge before you cook them. The more time you allow, the better they'll taste. Make sure they're well seasoned too. You could cut the wings in half to make winglets and roast them for 10–15 minutes. These are great served warm or cold.

ASIAN GLAZED GAMMON

FOR THE SPECIAL OCCASIONS OF CHRISTMAS AND EASTER, GAMMON IS SURE TO BE ON THE MENU I ENTERTAIN FOR MY EXTENDED FAMILY. IT'S THE FIRST DISH I SERVE WHEN THEY COME TO VISIT BECAUSE IT REALLY IS WONDERFUL, ESPECIALLY WITH ITS ASIAN-STYLE STOCK AND GLAZE.

PREPARATION TIME: 25 MIN
COOKING TIME: 1½ HRS
SERVES 6-8

1,5-2kg boneless gammon joint
500ml chicken stock
2 litres water (enough to cover)
2 dried bay leaves
6 cloves garlic, sliced
50ml fresh ginger, quartered
5ml black peppercorns
3 sprigs fresh thyme
3 sprigs rosemary
6 carrots, washed and cut into chunks
2 celery sticks, diced

GLAZE
30ml honey
45ml soy sauce
juice of ½ an orange
30ml fresh ginger, grated
3 cloves garlic, grated
1 red bird's eye chili

SERVE WITH
3 clementines, halved
spring onions, finely sliced lengthways

METHOD

Place the gammon in a large pot and cover with the stock and water. Add the bay leaves, garlic, ginger, peppercorns, thyme, rosemary, carrots and celery.

Bring to the boil and simmer for 30-45 minutes or until tender. Remove from the pot and leave to cool slightly.

Preheat the oven to 200°C. In a bowl, make the glaze by mixing the honey, soy sauce, orange juice, ginger and garlic. Slit open the bird's eye chili and add just a few of the seeds to the mix, discarding the rest of it.

Place the gammon on a roasting tray. Lightly score the fat and brush the glaze evenly over the meat. Place the clementines in the tray with the meat and brush with the glaze. Roast for 20-30 minutes until sticky and crisp round the edges. Garnish with the spring onions.

SCAN TO WATCH
A VIDEO ON
HOW TO
MAKE THIS RECIPE

Siba's tip...
If you use the QR code to watch the video of me making the gammon, please note the quantities aren't the same - this recipe has been adapted for a smaller yield. Make sure to increase the cooking time if you're cooking a bigger gammon, as in the video.

MEAT + POULTRY

ASIAN BEEF FILLET + CALAMARI

SURF AND TURF IS DEFINITELY A SIBA THING, ESPECIALLY WHEN ENTERTAINING. I CREATED THIS ROAST WHEN I HAD SPECIAL VISITORS FROM CHURCH, MOST OF WHOM WERE ORIGINALLY FROM AUSTRALIA. KNOWING THAT AUSTRALIAN CUISINE HAS A BIT OF AN ASIAN INFLUENCE, AND THAT ONE OF THE AUSSIES WAS A SURFER, I THOUGHT IT WOULD BE COOL TO SURF AND TURF ASIAN STYLE. THE MEAL WAS A TOTAL HIT AND EVEN THE KIDS LOVED IT. SO I'VE ADDED IT TO MY LIST OF GREAT, QUICK AND EASY-TO-EAT DINNERS.

PREPARATION TIME: 20 MIN
MARINATING TIME: 1–2 HRS
COOKING TIME: 30 MIN
SERVES 6–8

MARINADE
60ml sesame oil
90ml soy sauce
10ml rice wine vinegar
3 cloves garlic, crushed
10ml fresh ginger, grated
30ml coriander, chopped
2 spring onions, chopped
15ml honey or brown sugar
2ml chili flakes
5ml white sesame seeds

SURF + TURF
1kg beef fillet
80ml butter
2 cloves garlic
5ml fresh ginger, grated,
plus 2ml extra
1kg calamari cubes and heads,
rinsed and pat-dried
30ml fresh coriander, chopped,
plus extra to garnish
juice and zest of ½ lemon
250ml good-quality beef stock

METHOD

In a jug, whisk the marinade ingredients together until combined. Place the fillet in a freezer bag and pour two thirds of the marinade over it. Gently rub the meat and carefully seal the bag. Place it in a large dish and marinate in the fridge for an hour or two.

Preheat the oven to 200°C and lightly grease a roasting tin with cooking spray. Shake the marinade off the meat and pat it dry gently but thoroughly. Allow to rest for 5 minutes, to come to room temperature.

Heat a non-stick griddle pan until hot and sear the fillet for 2 minutes on each side until dark brown. Place on the prepared roasting tin, drizzle with oil and roast for 15–20 minutes until medium rare. Remove from the oven, place on a board and cover with foil, allowing to rest for 10 minutes.

For the calamari, heat half the butter in a large frying pan over a high heat and sauté the garlic and ginger. Add the calamari cubes and heads and cook for 2 minutes in batches, until cooked. Remove from the heat and stir in the coriander and a squeeze of lemon. Place on the board with the meat.

To make a sauce, heat the meat juices with the other half of the butter. Add the remaining third of the marinade and cook for 2 minutes. Pour in the stock and simmer until slightly reduced. Add the extra 2ml of ginger and cook a minute longer. Strain the sauce through a sieve into a serving jug. Serve with the meat and calamari, and garnish with coriander.

" **I LOVE** THE DISTINCT[...]
ON AN OPEN FIRE AND TH[...]
TASTE OF A BIT OF PAP D[...]
FEW THINGS MORE PLEAS[...]
REMINISCING AROUND A B[...]
FAMILY. IT SEEMS TO FULFIL[...]
DESIRES AND INSTINCTS. "

…VE SMELL OF MEAT COOKING
…E PECULIARLY SATISFYING
…PPED IN RELISH. THERE ARE
…NG THAN CHATTING AND
…AAI FIRE WITH FRIENDS AND
…SOME OF OUR MOST PRIMAL

PESTO-STUFFED LAMB RIB CHOPS

I LOVE THIS CARB-FREE MEAL AND MY FRIENDS WHO ARE BANTING ALWAYS APPRECIATE MY EFFORT TO CONSIDER THEIR PREFERENCES. IT'S A GREAT SURPRISE BITING INTO THESE LAMB RIB CHOPS AS THE STUFFING IS SO UNEXPECTED. I LIKE MINE COOKED MEDIUM WITH THE FAT SLIGHTLY CRISPY, BUT IF YOU PREFER YOURS MORE RARE, THEN JUST REDUCE THE COOKING TIME.

PREPARATION TIME: 15 MIN
COOKING TIME: 12 MIN
SERVES 4

12 lamb rib chops, frenched
2 cloves garlic, crushed
20ml homemade pesto
(see page 157 for recipe)
sea salt and freshly ground
black pepper
15 olive oil

STUFFING
60ml basil pesto
15ml pine nuts, toasted and very
roughly chopped
pinch of salt

COURGETTE 'PASTA'
15ml olive oil
2 cloves garlic, crushed
800g courgettes, cut using
a veg peeler with ridges
to make pasta spirals
6 sprigs thyme leaves
50g pine nuts, toasted, to serve
15ml basil leaves, to serve

METHOD

Make a slit on the fat side of the chops for the stuffing. Mix the garlic, pesto, salt and pepper together, and rub onto each chop on both sides. Using a teaspoon, mix the stuffing ingredients together and stuff a teaspoonful into the slit of each chop.

Heat a large non-stick pan, add the oil and wait until it's sizzling hot. Place the chops into the pan and cook for 3 minutes on each side, until medium. Cover with foil and set aside until serving time.

For the courgette 'pasta', heat the oil and sauté the garlic. Add the courgette spirals and cook for 3 minutes until just cooked, taking care not to overcook. Strip the thyme leaves from their stems and add to the pan and stir. Season with salt and pepper. Serve with the lamb chops, and top with toasted pine nuts and basil leaves.

SCAN TO WATCH
A VIDEO ON
HOW TO
MAKE THIS RECIPE

Siba's tip...
When frenching chops, I normally leave about 5cm of rib bone totally bare. This leaves the round of meat with a thin strip of fat on the side. Some people like to cut away so much that only a small 'lollipop' of meat is left. I, however, tend to be more generous, leaving all the meat and a little fat. This dish also goes well with the Cape Malay relish on page 158.

=107

SIBA'S SURF + TURF BRAAI

I LIKE TO SURF AND TURF FROM TIME TO TIME, ESPECIALLY WHEN BRAAING. THIS PORK CHOP AND TUNA STEAK COMBO IS AMAZING WITH MY VERY SPECIAL HOMEMADE MARINADE, WHICH CAN BE USED AS A BASTING SAUCE AND AS A SAUCE TO SERVE WITH THE MEAT. TAKE CARE NOT TO OVERCOOK YOUR TUNA STEAKS AS THEY REALLY DO COOK SO QUICKLY.

PREPARATION TIME: 15 MIN
COOKING TIME: 15 MIN
SERVES 6

200ml sweet soy sauce
(Ketjap manis, if possible)
200ml sticky dark brown sugar
90ml olive oil
120ml fresh ginger, peeled and
roughly sliced
10 cloves garlic, peeled
45ml tomato purée
500ml warm water
juice and zest of 1 lemon
60ml fresh thyme,
stems removed
2 whole red bird's eye chilies,
slightly split
6 x 120g tuna steaks
6 pork chops
large handful fresh sage leaves
1 bottle beer lager (optional)
cucumber ribbons, to garnish
micro herbs, to garnish

MEAT + POULTRY

METHOD

Place the soy sauce, sugar, olive oil, ginger, garlic and tomato paste into a food processor and blitz to a paste. Add the water and blitz again until well combined. Pour into a frying pan and bring to a simmer.

Add the lemon juice and zest, thyme and chilies and simmer the mixture for another 5 minutes, until it thickens and reduces slightly. Remove from the heat and leave to cool. Once cooled, transfer to a measuring jug so it's easy to pour. Remove and discard the chilies.

Place the tuna steaks and pork chops into separate large resealable freezer bags. Pour half of the cooled marinade in with the tuna steaks and the other half in with the pork. Place the sage leaves in the bag with the pork chops and gently rub.

Make sure everything is completely coated before sealing both bags and placing in the fridge to marinate. When ready to braai, remove the tuna and pork from their bags and shake off the excess marinade.

Grill the pork chops on the braai for 3-4 minutes on each side, until cooked. Drizzle the beer, if using, over the pork while cooking, for an authentic South African braai flavour. Braai the tuna steaks for 1 minute a side or longer, depending on how you like them. Garnish with cucumber ribbons and micro herbs before serving.

SCAN TO WATCH
A VIDEO ON
HOW TO
MAKE THIS RECIPE

Siba's tip...
To ensure that your tuna is lovely and pink on the inside, you can also use one big piece of fish that's equal in weight to the individual steak pieces (680g), and marinate it, cook it whole and slice it afterwards. Whichever way you choose, this surf and turf is a winner!

STEAK WITH SPICY TOMATO RELISH

GROWING UP IN THE EASTERN CAPE, IN MDANTSANE, WE SELDOM HAD DINNER WITHOUT SOME FORM OF INYAMA (MEAT). A MEAL SIMPLY FELT INCOMPLETE WITHOUT IT. BACK THEN, BEING ABLE TO AFFORD MEAT ON A DAILY BASIS WAS, TO A CERTAIN EXTENT, A SIGN OF AFFLUENCE. MY DAD REALLY ENJOYED THIS DISH, AS LONG AS IT WAS WELL DONE. IT'S REALLY TASTY, WHETHER GRILLED ON THE STOVE OR BRAAIED ON COALS, AND THE RELISH IS A PERFECT MATCH.

PREPARATION TIME: 10 MIN
COOKING TIME: 25 MIN
SERVES 4

2 x 500g rump steak, ideally 3cm thick rather than wide
15ml olive oil

RUB
15ml garlic, crushed
6 sprigs fresh thyme leaves
5ml smoked sea salt
5ml freshly ground black pepper

RELISH
15ml oil
5ml garlic, crushed
4 spring onions, chopped
5ml smoked paprika
400g can tomatoes, with added basil and oregano
2ml smoked sea salt
2ml freshly ground black pepper
2ml white sugar
micro greens, to garnish

METHOD

Heat a non-stick griddle pan until hot over high heat. Drizzle the olive oil all over the steaks and gently rub it in. Then mix the rub ingredients together to form a paste and rub that over the steaks. Place the steaks on a very hot griddle for about 4–6 minutes a side for medium rare. This will depend on the thickness of the steak.

Remove the steak from the heat, cover and allow to rest for 5 minutes. When the steak has rested, cut it across the grain in slices. Serve on a large plate or board with the relish alongside it.

For the relish, heat the oil and sauté the garlic and spring onion for 2 minutes until soft. Add the paprika and cook for a minute. Add the can of tomatoes and simmer for 15 minutes until the relish thickens. Season with salt, pepper and sugar, to taste. Garnish with micro greens and serve.

SCAN TO WATCH
A VIDEO ON
HOW TO
MAKE THIS RECIPE

Siba's tip...
Serve with potato or sweet potato mash, or with a warm side of roasted vegetables or salad. Note that in the video, I use one large piece of steak, which takes longer to cook

COBB SALAD BURGER

Since we often have homemade burgers at home, I like to vary them a bit with a twist of my own. In this recipe, I've taken the ingredients normally used to make an American cobb salad and turned them into this wonderful burger. Stuffing the chicken with blue cheese is absolutely fantastic and gives the burger an additional flavour that perfectly matches the cobb salad ingredients.

PREPARATION TIME: 20 MIN
COOKING TIME: 15 MIN
SERVES 2

2 chicken breasts
30ml Roquefort or blue cheese
4 cocktail sticks

WET RUB
15ml cumin
15ml brown sugar
5ml mild curry powder
5ml cayenne powder
5ml Dijon mustard
2 cloves garlic, chopped
15ml canola oil
15ml apple cider vinegar
salt and black pepper

4 rashers bacon
30ml maple syrup
2 large eggs
2 sesame-seed sourdough rolls

SERVE WITH
150g mixed baby lettuce leaves
4 slices tomato, sliced
1 avocado, halved and sliced
1 small red onion, roughly sliced

METHOD

Make a small slit on one side of each chicken breast, stuff it with the blue cheese and secure with a cocktail stick. Mix the rub ingredients together and rub all over the chicken. Heat the butter and cook the chicken for 5-6 minutes on each side, until cooked through. Set aside to rest for 5 minutes.

On a hot griddle pan, cook the bacon rashers for 5 minutes each side, until they start to brown. Brush maple syrup on both sides and cook for another minute on each side, until they caramelise a little. Allow to cool and crispen.

To boil the eggs so that they are soft, place them in a small saucepan, cover with cold water and bring to the boil. Remove the saucepan from the heat and allow the eggs to stand for 5 minutes in the boiled water. Remove from the saucepan using a slotted spoon and peel under cold, running water.

Halve, toast and butter the rolls and place them on a larger platter. Top each half with lettuce, tomato and red onion slices. Then top two of them with the stuffed chicken and bacon strips, and the other two with the avocado and egg. Drizzle with ranch dressing (see recipe on page 167) and serve.

Siba's tip...
When making the slit on the side of the chicken breasts, take care not to pierce through to the other side, otherwise the stuffing will ooze out when cooking. If using the oven to cook the bacon rashers, place them on a baking sheet and bake at 200°C for about 15 minutes until they start to brown. Brush them with maple syrup and give them another 5 minutes, then take them out to cool and crispen. To toast the rolls on a hot griddle pan, place them buttered side down for 3-4 minutes until golden and crispy.

MEAT + POULTRY

=113

Sibalicious!

HMMM!

ndiyayithanda inyama

(I love meat)

RIBS

STICKY RIBS ARE A FRIDAY THING AT HOME AND MY BOYS LOVE THEM. MY ELDER SON, LONWABO, SOMETIMES LIKES THEM DUNKED IN THE MARINADE EVEN THOUGH IT HAS A HINT OF CHILI IN IT. I THINK IT'S SO CUTE WHEN HE SAYS, 'IYABABA MAMA' WHICH MEANS 'IT'S HOT MUM', BUT DUNKS ANOTHER ONE ANYWAY, AND I SUPPOSE FOR HIS INNOCENT PALATE IT IS A BIT HOT. FOR A MORE DEVELOPED ONE, THE HEAT OF THE CHILI IS REALLY JUST A HINT IN THE BACKGROUND.

PREPARATION TIME: 15 MIN
COOKING TIME: 40 MIN
SERVES 4-6

1,5kg pork ribs, rinsed
and pat-dried

MARINADE
125ml soy sauce
160ml honey
60ml soft brown sugar
3cm fresh ginger, grated
4 cloves garlic, crushed
5ml cayenne pepper
5ml ground cumin
1 red chili, deseeded, pith
removed and chopped
water, to cover

GARNISH
spring onion, sliced
fresh coriander
1 small lemon, charred

METHOD

Place the ribs in a large saucepan and set aside. In a jug, mix all the marinade ingredients together and stir well to combine. Pour over the ribs, cover with warm water and bring to the boil. Reduce the heat and simmer for 30-40 minutes, until the ribs are cooked and the marinade has significantly reduced.

Set the oven to grill at 230°C or set it on grill. Remove the ribs from the pan, place on a wooden board and cut into riblets.

Place on a baking tray and baste with the thickened marinade. Grill in the oven on the top rack for 10 minutes, keeping a close watch that they don't burn, turning them if necessary. Remove from the oven and place on a platter. Garnish with the fresh coriander, spring onions and a squeeze of the charred lemon.

Siba's tip...
Once the ribs are in the oven grilling, they can burn very quickly, so it helps to open the oven door slightly, both to reduce the heat and to have a clear view of them as they cook.

ZA'ATAR CHICKEN + LEMON KEBABS

I FELL IN LOVE WITH ZA'ATAR WHILE TRAVELLING IN THE MIDDLE EAST. SOME RETAIL STORES AND SPECIALTY FOOD STORES CARRY IT LOCALLY, BUT IT'S VERY EASY TO MAKE YOUR OWN TOO. ITS MAIN INGREDIENT, THE DEEP RED AND QUITE SOUR SUMAC SPICE, ALSO AVAILABLE LOCALLY, IS MIXED WITH A SELECTION OF DRIED HERBS, WITH THYME BEING THE MOST DOMINANT. ZA'ATAR GOES WELL WITH A VARIETY OF MEATS, CHICKEN AND EVEN FISH.

PREPARATION TIME: 15 MIN
COOKING TIME: 10 MIN
SERVES 4

4 skinless chicken fillets, cubed
20ml za'atar
2 cloves garlic, crushed
20ml olive oil
8 wooden or metal skewers
2 lemons, thinly sliced

ZA'ATAR BUTTER SAUCE
60ml butter
1 clove garlic, crushed
15ml za'atar

SERVE WITH
8 store-bought mini
pitas, warmed
250g tomatoes on the
vine, pan-fried
1 lemon, quartered, to garnish
80ml tzatziki (see recipe on
page 162)
sprig of fresh dill, to garnish

METHOD

Cut each chicken fillet in half lengthways, and then across three times, to create 8 cubes (4 cubes per kebab and 2 kebabs per person).

Combine the za'atar, garlic and olive oil and pour over the chicken cubes. Toss to combine. Thread the cubes onto wooden or metal skewers, with a folded slice of lemon between each piece.

Heat the griddle pan and cook the chicken for 6–8 minutes, 3–4 minutes on each side, rotating and pressing down the skewers to make sure the chicken cooks evenly. Remove from the heat, place on a platter and cover with foil.

Heat the butter and sauté the garlic for a minute. Add the za'atar and cook until the butter is golden brown, with a nutty smell and taste. Remove the foil and pour the butter sauce over the kebabs. Serve with the warm pitas, pan-fried tomatoes, lemon wedges and tzatziki, and garnish with the dill.

SCAN TO WATCH
A VIDEO ON
HOW TO
MAKE THIS RECIPE

Siba's tip...

To make your own za'atar, mix 15ml sumac, 15ml dried thyme, 15ml dried oregano, 5ml white sesame seeds, 5ml back sesame seeds, 2ml sea salt and 2 crushed garlic cloves or 5ml garlic flakes together and grind using a pestle and mortar, until fine. If you plan to keep this mix for a long time, in a sealed container, then it's best to use garlic flakes rather than fresh garlic.

SWEET + SOUR KEBABS

For these kebabs, I use a Cape Malay-inspired marinade, and I often make them for potluck gatherings with close friends and family. It works so well when guests contribute, making it easier for the person hosting the get-together and everyone feels they've played a part in making the gathering special.

METHOD

First prick the meat right through. Cut the steaks in half lengthways and across three times, so that each steak yields eight pieces.

Now thread the meat onto the skewers with the halved apricots, red peppers and onions and place them in a large, deep dish or resealable freezer bag. Pour the marinade over the kebabs and rub the marinade into the meat. Marinate for 2 hours in the fridge.

Heat the oil in a grill pan and grill the kebabs for 4 minutes on each side (for medium rare), turning continuously. Allow the meat to rest, wrapped in foil, for at least 5 minutes before serving it. Garnish with a few sprigs of bay leaves.

PREPARATION TIME: 5 MIN
MARINATING TIME: 2 HRS
COOKING TIME: 8 MIN
MAKES 8 KEBABS

4 sirloin steaks
8 metal skewers
8 Turkish dried apricots, cut in
half lengthways
2 large red peppers, cored
and cubed
1 red onion, cut into
squared slices
250ml Cape Malay marinade
(see recipe on page 158)
15ml vegetable oil
sprigs of bay leaves, to garnish

Siba's tip...
This also goes well with the Cape Malay relish on page 158.

STUFFED PORK ROAST

NOTHING TASTES QUITE AS GOOD AS THE STUFFED PORK ROAST YOU'LL MAKE WITH THIS RECIPE. THE CRACKLING IS WONDERFUL! I OFTEN SERVE IT WITH APPLE GRAVY, ROUGHLY MASHED SWEET POTATOES AND GREENS. THIS IS A SUPER STAR THAT WILL DELIGHT BOTH YOUR FAMILY AND DINNER GUESTS.

PREPARATION TIME: 20 MIN
COOKING TIME: 1H45 MIN
SERVES 6+

30ml olive oil, plus extra to grease
4 bacon rashers
1 large onion, finely chopped
2 cloves garlic, crushed
30ml sage, chopped
400g bunch spinach, stems removed, thoroughly washed, pat-dried and chopped
250ml dried breadcrumbs
sea salt and black pepper, to taste

PORK
1.5kg boned, butterflied pork leg
10ml sea salt, to rub
6 pears, halved (optional)

APPLE GRAVY
30ml butter
4 apples, peeled and cored
180ml apple juice or white wine
30ml apple cider vinegar
250ml chicken stock
5ml Dijon mustard
5ml whole-grain mustard
salt and black pepper, to taste
15ml brown sugar, to taste

METHOD

Preheat the oven to 220°C and lightly grease a roasting pan with oil. Heat half the oil in a large frying pan and cook the bacon rashers for about 5 minutes, until slightly crispy. Add the chopped onion and sauté for 3 minutes. Add the garlic and the sage, and cook for 1 minute.

Add the spinach and breadcrumbs and cook until the spinach has wilted slightly. Season with salt and pepper. On a clean flat surface, place the meat with the skin-side down. Place the stuffing in the centre and tightly roll the meat to enclose the stuffing. Secure the roll with kitchen string every 2cm.

Rub the pork with the remaining oil and sea salt. Heat the oil in a large frying pan. Brown the outside of the meat, turning it until it's crispy all round. Transfer to the roasting pan, pop the pears in with the meat, if using, and roast in the oven for 40 minutes. Reduce the heat to 180°C and cook for a further 30–45 minutes until the pork is tender and cooked.

Transfer to a serving platter, cover with foil and allow to rest for 15 minutes. You'll remove the string just before serving. While the meat is resting, prepare the apple gravy. In a large saucepan, heat the butter and sauté the apples for 2 minutes. Pour in the apple juice, apple cider vinegar and chicken stock, stirring until mixed.

Simmer for 5 minutes, until it has reduced. Add the Dijon and whole-grain mustards and the pork's pan juices, and season with salt and pepper and a bit of sugar. Simmer for 10 minutes over a medium heat. Remove from the heat and strain through a sieve into a serving jug. Serve with the meat.

TERIYAKI CHICKEN

CHICKEN IS ONE OF THE MOST VERSATILE, CONVENIENT AND REASONABLY PRICED MEATS AVAILABLE. IT'S EASY AND RELATIVELY QUICK TO COOK. THESE CHICKEN FILLETS, WHICH ARE DONE IN JUST 15 MINUTES, ARE A PERFECT EXAMPLE. I ALWAYS VARY THE FLAVOURS OF OUR CHICKEN MEALS SO THEY DON'T BECOME BORING. THIS ONE HAS A JAPANESE INFLUENCE AND IS REALLY DELICIOUS.

PREPARATION TIME: 20 MIN
COOKING TIME: 10 MIN
SERVES 4

4 chicken breasts, skinned and boned
10ml fresh ginger, grated
2 cloves garlic, crushed
pinch of sea salt

SAUCE
60ml sake
60ml mirin
60ml soy sauce
30ml honey
30ml sesame oil, plus 30ml extra for frying
5ml fresh ginger, grated
1 clove garlic, crushed
2ml chili flakes

SERVE WITH
3 clementines
25ml butter
60ml sticky brown sugar
25ml unsalted butter
cooked basmati rice
15ml fresh coriander leaves
15ml sesame seeds, toasted

METHOD

Score the chicken fillets with a sharp knife and rub them with the garlic, ginger and salt, making sure to rub the inner, scored parts of the meat. Place in a deep dish and set aside.

Meanwhile, mix the sauce ingredients in a small jug and pour the mixture over the chicken. Leave the chicken in the sauce for about 15 minutes. Heat a large non-stick frying pan and add the extra sesame oil. Remove the chicken breasts from the sauce and cook them, with the scored-side down, for 3 minutes before turning.

Pour the sauce over the chicken and cook until the sauce thickens slightly and the chicken is cooked through. Take care not to overcook it, as it will become dry.

In a large pan, pan-fry the clementines in the melted butter and sugar until golden brown and set aside.

Serve the chicken with the rice and pan-seared clementines. Garnish with the fresh coriander and sesame seeds.

Siba's tip...
Sake is a clear Japanese rice wine that's made from fermented polished rice (rice without bran) and is very popular in Asian cooking. Mirin is also a rice wine, similar to sake but with a lower alcohol content and a much higher sugar content. Together with soy sauce, these rice wines are the key teriyaki ingredients. This sauce is used for marinating and cooking the chicken here, but it's also good with fish and pork. If you can't find the rice wines in your local supermarket, try Asian or Chinese supermarkets or restaurants.

SOY, HONEY + MUSTARD CHICKEN SALAD

THIS IS A SALAD WITH SUBSTANCE. I OFTEN MAKE IT FOR LUNCH WHEN I HAVE FRIENDS OVER AND WANT SOMETHING SIMPLE BUT ELEGANT AND TASTY. THE INGREDIENTS COMPLEMENT EACH OTHER SO WELL AND I LIKE BEING ABLE TO USE THE SAUCE IN THREE WAYS — AS A MARINADE, A COOK-IN SAUCE AND A DRESSING — AS IT SAVES ME A LOT OF TIME.

PREPARATION: 15 MIN
COOKING: 10 MIN
MARINATING TIME: 2 HRS
SERVES 4

4 chicken fillets

MARINADE
30ml soy sauce
60ml honey
15ml whole-grain mustard
5ml Dijon mustard
1 clove garlic
2ml chili flakes
30ml oil

SERVE WITH
bacon wrapped greens
(see recipe on page 55)
250g mixed baby salad leaves
1 heirloom tomatoes, sliced
Parmesan shavings

METHOD

Lightly score the chicken fillets and place them in a large dish. Mix the marinade ingredients together, except for the oil, and pour two thirds of it onto the chicken, reserving the other third for the dressing. Marinate for 2 hours or more.

Heat the oil in a large pan and cook the marinated chicken fillets for about 4 minutes on each side, until cooked. Remove from the heat and pour the pan juices over them. Cover with foil and allow to rest for 5 minutes. Cut into slices.

To serve, arrange the bacon wrapped greens on a platter with the chicken, baby salad leaves and tomato slices. Sprinkle with Parmesan shavings and drizzle with the reserved soy, honey and mustard marinade, as a dressing.

Siba's tip...

Heirloom tomatoes are becoming increasingly popular. Unlike most tomatoes we buy or even plant, they are not hybrids and do not have the uniform red appearance. They usually have a shorter shelf life, and come in a variety of 'imperfect' shapes, sizes and colours. The consensus is that they taste far better than their hybrid cousins.

MAKE THE RIGHT CHOICES

Making sustainable seafood choices is important. In this book, there are recipes using prawns, which are on the WWF Orange List. Where Tuna and Salmon are indicated, please try to choose species that are not on the endangered list. As this list changes all the time, I suggest that you regularly refer to the WWF seafood guides online. If you are in SA click on SASSI (South African Sustainable Seafood Initiative).

SEAFO

Whenever I can't decide what to cook,
I turn to fish ... tasty, healthy, easy ...

OOD

OYSTERS!

THIS WONDERFUL DRESSING IS DERIVED FROM THE OYSTERS A VERY GOOD FRIEND ONCE SERVED US.
I LOVED THE PUNGENT FLAVOURS AND THE TINGE OF RED FROM THE POMEGRANATE RUBIES AND THE
GARNISH OF FRESH CORIANDER.

PREPARATION TIME: 10 MIN
NO COOKING TIME
SERVES 4-6

SALSA

1 small shallot onion, very
finely chopped
80ml raspberry vinegar
15ml white sugar
a splash of olive oil
60ml pomegranate rubies, plus
extra to garnish

OYSTERS

1 litre bag of ice, crushed
sea salt
12 oysters, defrosted if not fresh
15ml fresh coriander, to garnish

METHOD

Mix the chopped shallot, vinegar, sugar, a splash of olive oil and pomegranate rubies together in a jug and set aside. On a serving platter, layer the crushed ice and sprinkle the sea salt over it. (Salt prevents the ice from melting too quickly.) Arrange the oysters on top.

Spoon a little dressing over each oyster and garnish with the extra pomegranate rubies and coriander.

Siba's tip...
The great thing about this dressing is that it can be made in advance and stored in the fridge until serving time. If the oysters are frozen, it's best to defrost them overnight in the fridge. Make sure they're in a closed container so that they don't drip onto, and contaminate, other food in the fridge. Arrange the oysters as close to your guests' arrival as possible so the ice doesn't melt away before you serve them. Keep in a cool area, away from direct sunlight. Shallots are the smaller, oval-shaped onions, which are milder and have more of a subtle, sweet taste. They're great in vinaigrettes and egg dishes, and in this salad they complement the oysters very well.

CREAMY MUSSELS WITH COURGETTE 'PASTA'

THE FIRST TIME I SUGGESTED COOKING CREAMY MUSSELS FOR MY MOTHER, I WAS REALLY SURPRISED WHEN SHE EXCITEDLY AGREED. SHE THEN TOLD ME THE STORY OF HOW, AS A YOUNG GIRL IN THE RURAL PARTS OF THE BEAUTIFUL EASTERN CAPE, SHE WOULD ACCOMPANY HER AUNT TO THE BEACH. THERE THEY WOULD PICK MUSSELS — IMBAZA IN XHOSA — OFF THE ROCKS AT LOW TIDE. THEY WOULD THEN MAKE A SMALL FIRE AND COOK THE MUSSELS IN LARGE TINS, WAITING UNTIL THEY OPENED BEFORE DIGGING IN.

PREPARATION: 15 MIN
COOKING: 10 MIN
SERVES 4

30ml olive oil
15ml butter
2 cloves garlic, crushed
4 spring onions, sliced
30ml fresh chives, chopped
5ml fresh thyme, chopped
8 large courgettes, sliced into long thin strips using a vegetable peeler

MUSSELS
2 cloves garlic, crushed
15ml garlic butter
2ml mustard powder
15ml whole-grain mustard
125ml good-quality chicken stock
180ml milk
30ml crème fraîche
1,5kg mussels, thoroughly cleaned

METHOD

Heat the oil and butter in a large saucepan and sauté the garlic for 1 minute. Add the spring onions, chives and thyme and cook for a further minute. Add the courgette strips and stir-fry for 2–4 minutes, until al dente, taking care not to overcook them. Set aside.

To make the mussels, sauté the garlic in the garlic butter for 1 minute. Add the mustard powder and whole-grain mustard and stir for about 30 seconds. Pour in the stock and milk and bring to the boil. Add the crème fraîche and stir until dissolved.

Add the mussels and cook for 2–4 minutes, or until they open. Discard any that don't. Serve with the courgette 'pasta'.

Siba's tip...
It's important to wash mussels thoroughly before cooking them. Scrub them with a brush under running water to remove the sand and pull off the beard, and only cook the ones that are tightly closed. If any open up while being washed, discard them.

STUFFED + BAKED SALMON

MY HUSBAND AND I LOVE EATING OUT BUT THAT BECAME A BIT TRICKY WHEN LONWABO AND LINAMANDLA ARRIVED. SO, WE CAME UP WITH A PLAN TO ENJOY A WEEKLY ROMANTIC DINNER FOR TWO, AT HOME. OUR DATE NIGHT IS ON A THURSDAY AND I USUALLY COOK SOMETHING SPECIAL, WHILE BRIAN'S DUTY IS TO BRING HOME A LITTLE PRESENT. THIS DISH IS A DATE-NIGHT SPECIAL THAT NOW MAKES A REGULAR APPEARANCE BECAUSE MY WHOLE FAMILY LOVES IT.

PREPARATION TIME: 15 MIN
COOKING TIME: 20 MIN
SERVES 2

30ml olive oil
2 cloves garlic, crushed
100g mushrooms, sliced
½ red pepper, sliced
100g Swiss chard or spinach
15ml fresh thyme, chopped
zest of ½ lemon
sea salt and freshly ground
black pepper
2 x 250g fresh salmon fillets,
skin off
140g sugar snaps
juice of a lemon wedge
micro herbs, to garnish

METHOD

Preheat the oven to 200°C and lightly grease a baking tray with cooking spray. Heat the oil in a large non-stick frying pan and sauté the garlic for a minute. Add the mushrooms and cook over high heat for 4 minutes until slightly soft. Add the red pepper and cook for another 2 minutes.

Next add the Swiss chard, thyme and lemon zest and cook for about 3-4 minutes until wilted. Season and leave the stuffing to cool.

Make a lengthways slit on the fish fillets to make room for the stuffing. Stuff each fillet and place them on a baking sheet. Lightly season and bake for 10 minutes.

Add the sugar snaps and bake for a further 2 minutes until the fish flakes when tested with a fork and the veggies are lightly cooked but still crunchy. The fish should be pink inside.

Transfer to a serving platter, finish with a squeeze of lemon juice and garnish with micro herbs. Serve while still warm.

SCAN TO WATCH
A VIDEO ON
HOW TO
MAKE THIS RECIPE

Siba's tip...
Take care not to overcook the veggies, especially the red pepper and Swiss chard (or spinach). Because the fish is stuffed, it will also cook a lot quicker. So keep an eye on it.

SEARED TUNA + WHEAT SALAD

THIS IS A VERY OLD RECIPE THAT I MADE WHEN I WAS A FULLTIME MAGAZINE FOOD EDITOR.
I USED CANNED TUNA THEN, BUT HAVE SINCE DECIDED THAT FRESH TUNA WORKS EVEN BETTER.

PREPARATION TIME: 25 MIN
WAITING TIME: 30 MIN
COOKING TIME: 35 MIN
SERVES 4

250ml crushed wheat
salted water, to cover

TUNA
2 cloves garlic, chopped
30ml parsley, chopped
30ml coriander, chopped
zest of 1 lemon
2ml cayenne pepper
salt and freshly ground black pepper
200-400g fresh tuna steak

DRESSING
80ml olive oil
juice of ½ or 1 lemon
20ml soy sauce
freshly ground black pepper, to taste
15ml fresh parsley, chopped
honey or sugar, to taste

SALAD
1 cucumber, cubed and seeds removed
250g cherry tomatoes, ha lved
40ml spring onions, thinly sliced
125ml fresh parsley, roughly chopped

METHOD

Soak the crushed wheat in cold water for 30 minutes to allow the grains to swell, then drain. Place in a saucepan, cover with salted water and bring to the boil. Cook for 30 minutes until tender. Drain and strain under cold running water and drain again.

Mix the garlic, herbs, lemon zest, cayenne pepper and seasoning and rub on the tuna. Heat the oil until hot and sear the tuna for 4 minutes in total all around. Cut into slices.

Combine the dressing ingredients and stir well. Mix the crushed wheat and all the salad ingredients in a large bowl and drizzle half the salad dressing over it. Toss well.

Arrange on a platter and top with the tuna slices. Drizzle with the remaining dressing and serve immediately.

Siba's tip...

This salad also works well with barley or wild quinoa or half of each, instead of the crushed wheat. Keep tasting the dressing as you make it to be sure you've added enough honey or sugar to balance the sharp, sour taste of the lemon juice.

"I LOVE FISH. IT'S

CAN BE STYLISH, MYSTERIO

PREHISTORIC CHARM OF MU

PRAWNS, OCTOPUS AND

SALMON, TUNA AND CAV

SIMPLICITY OF A PARCEL OF

SO VERSATILE BECAUSE IT
S AND HOMELY. THINK OF THE
SELS, OYSTERS, SCALLOPS,
RAYFISH; THE LUXURY OF
AR; AND THE SATISFYING
FISH AND CHIPS."

HERBED BUTTER SAUCE PRAWNS WITH COUSCOUS

THIS HERBED BUTTER SAUCE IS SCRUMPTIOUS AND GOES WELL WITH ALL SEAFOOD, ESPECIALLY GRILLED CALAMARI RINGS AND GRILLED FISH.

PREPARATION TIME: 15 MIN
COOKING TIME: 10 MIN
SERVES 4

340ml couscous
boiling water or
chicken stock, to cover

BUTTER SAUCE + PRAWNS
80ml butter
4 cloves garlic, crushed
10ml ginger, finely grated
10ml fresh thyme
60ml coriander, roughly chopped
1 fresh red chili, seeded and chopped
juice and zest of 1–2 lemons
800g fresh prawns, shelled

SALAD
2 cloves garlic, crushed
120g fresh peas
100g asparagus tips, rinsed
30ml fresh coriander, chopped
30ml fresh parsley, roughly chopped
30ml mint, roughly chopped
pinch of sea salt and freshly ground
black pepper, to taste
60ml wild rocket
mint leaves, to garnish
spring onions, to garnish

METHOD

Prepare the couscous by placing it in a large deep dish and covering it with boiling water or chicken stock. Cover with plastic wrap and leave for about 15 minutes until the granules have doubled in size.

To make the butter sauce, fry the butter, garlic, ginger, herbs and chili in a large non-stick frying pan for 2 minutes. Add the zest and lemon juice and stir. Cook the prawns in a third of the sauce for 4 minutes and set aside.

To make the salad, heat another third of the butter sauce in a pan over a medium heat. Add the garlic and cook for 30 seconds. Add the peas and asparagus tips and cook for 2 minutes. Add the herbs, season with salt and pepper and stir. Remove from the heat and allow to cool slightly.

Fluff the couscous with a fork, then stir in the pea and asparagus mixture. Toss in the wild rocket, transfer to a serving platter and serve with the prawns and remaining third of the butter sauce. Garnish with mint leaves and spring onions.

Siba's tip...
Check the couscous package for cooking instructions as one brand differs from another in terms of quantities and swelling times. Using chicken stock instead of water adds a tasty savoury flavour. Be sure though not to season the dish with too much salt and pepper as the chicken stock is already quite salty.

SEAFOOD

TEX-MEX SALMON

I LOVE THESE FLAVOURS AND THE POP-IN-YOUR-MOUTH FEELING WHEN YOU BITE INTO THE WHOLE CHERRY TOMATOES. I USED TO DO A VERSION OF THIS RECIPE AS A BRAAI BEFORE. I WOULD WRAP THE FISH IN TINFOIL, PLACE IT ON THE COALS AND ADD A FEW COALS ON TOP OF THE PARCEL. THIS METHOD ALWAYS MAKES ME THINK OF A TIME WHEN I WAS A YOUNG GIRL IN THE RURAL PARTS OF THE EASTERN CAPE. I USED TO WATCH THE OLDER WOMEN DIG A HOLE IN THE GROUND AND PILE COAL INTO IT, THEN PLACE A POT INSIDE AND COVER IT WITH COALS. THIS REALLY FASCINATED ME. THE BAKED VERSION IS FOR THOSE OCCASIONS ON WHICH YOU WANT TO STAY INDOORS AND USE A STOVE.

PREPARATION TIME: 10 MIN
COOKING TIME: 20-30 MIN
SERVES 4-6

800g-1kg salmon fillet, pin bones removed and skin left on
sea salt and freshly ground black pepper, to taste
80ml butter
20ml seafood rub, to taste
3 cloves garlic, crushed
handful fresh sage, roughly chopped
3 small red onions, roughly sliced
200g cherry tomatoes

METHOD

Preheat the oven to 200°C and line a baking tray with baking paper. Place the fish fillet on the prepared tray and rub with garlic, salt and pepper.

Dot with the butter and sprinkle with the seafood rub. Scatter the sage, onions and tomatoes over the fish and dot with the remaining butter. Leave a few sage leaves aside for garnishing.

Place in the oven and cook for 20-30 minutes until the salmon flakes when pressed in the thickest part. The flesh should still be pink inside, otherwise it's too dry.

SEAFOOD

SCAN TO WATCH
A VIDEO ON
HOW TO
MAKE THIS RECIPE

Siba's tip...
You can make your own seafood rub using sea salt, onion powder, garlic flakes, mustard seeds, crushed coriander seeds, crushed bay leaves, black pepper, lemon zest and dried herbs such as thyme, chili, oregano, basil and parsley.

FISH + CHIPS

HAVING SPENT MOST OF MY ADULT LIFE IN CAPE TOWN, THE MOTHER CITY AS WE CALL IT, WHERE 'VIS EN TJIPS' HAS FOR GENERATIONS BEEN AVAILABLE AT EVERY TURN, I FIND IT HARD TO BELIEVE THAT THE COMBO HAS ITS ORIGINS IN ENGLAND. I ACTUALLY PREFER MY FISH PAN-FRIED IN A LITTLE OIL OR BUTTER OR BAKED OR GRILLED, BUT THERE ARE OCCASIONS WHEN FRIED FISH AND CHIPS AT HOME ACCOMPANIED BY ONE OF MY SAUCES SUCH AS TARTAR, GARLIC, SEAFOOD AND PERI-PERI, IS JUST WHAT I FEEL LIKE.

PREPARATION TIME: 10 MIN
COOKING TIME: 15 MIN
SERVES 4

4 x 400g hake fillets
sea salt

BEER BATTER
250ml seasoned all-purpose flour, plus extra
15ml baking powder
1 x 330ml cold beer
vegetable oil for deep-frying

CHIPS
4 large potatoes, cut into wedges

METHOD

Place the fish on a flat clean surface and season with the sea salt. To make the beer batter, mix the seasoned flour, baking powder and cold beer together in a large bowl and whisk well until lump free.

Now heat the oil in a large deep pan until hot. Dip the fish in the beer batter, drip the excess off and fry in the oil for about 5–6 minutes until cooked and the batter is gold and crispy.

Remove the fish with a slotted spoon and place on a plate with absorbent paper. Fish out the batter-crumb bits in the oil with a spoon and repeat with the remaining fillets.

Heat the oil again, season the potato wedges and fry in batches for 4–6 minutes or until cooked and golden brown.

Siba's tip...
The oil needs to be hot enough to fry in, otherwise the batter will absorb too much of it and result in heavy and greasy fish. Unless you're using a deep-fryer where temperature levels can be monitored, you can check that your oil is the right temperature by placing a little breadcrumb in it. If the oil is hot enough the crumb will float to the surface and brown to a golden colour fairly quickly. If the oil isn't yet hot enough, the crumb will sink and take a while to float to the surface and brown.

BAKED SALMON STEAK PARCELS

I LOVE THE SIMPLE FLAVOURS OF THIS DISH AND THE FACT THAT IT'S SERVED IN THE PARCHMENT PARCEL IT'S BAKED IN. IT'S A BIT OF A NOVELTY TO HAVE YOUR GUESTS UNWRAPPING THEIR PARCELS THEMSELVES.

PREPARATION TIME: 10 MIN
COOKING TIME: 25 MIN
SERVES 2

2 x 250g salmon steaks
smoked sea salt and freshly
ground black pepper
2 pieces of parchment, 40x40cm
250g cherry tomatoes
1 small onion, halved and sliced
1 yellow pepper, sliced
30ml fresh dill, chopped
30ml butter, melted
1 lime, halved

METHOD

Preheat the oven to 200°C. Season the salmon steaks with salt and pepper and place each one on a large sheet of parchment that's been laid out on a baking tray. (If you don't have parchment, you can use tinfoil. Parchment is just prettier.)

Top with the tomatoes, onion slices, yellow pepper and a sprinkle of dill. Drizzle the butter and a squeeze of half a lime over each. Fold the parchment over and seal the edges tightly.

Making sure the parchment parcels don't touch the top grill element, place in the oven and bake for 15 minutes until cooked. (The fish should flake when touched and still be pink inside.) Place each parcel on a warmed dinner plate and serve with a salad or mash, or both.

SCAN TO WATCH
A VIDEO ON
HOW TO
MAKE THIS RECIPE

If I ever have to go to a desert island, I'll pack my box of spices first.

DIPS

RUBS MARINADES PASTES & dressings

red pepper
hummus

roasted
butternut
hummus

baba ghanoush

THESE THREE DIPS ARE MOSTLY INSPIRED BY THE MIDDLE EAST AND THEY'RE HANDY TO SERVE ALONGSIDE CANAPÉS AND CRUDITÉS WHEN HOSTING A LARGE NUMBER OF PEOPLE. THEY'RE ALL QUICK AND EASY TO MAKE AS THE BLENDER DOES MOST OF THE WORK, APART FROM THE ROASTED BUTTERNUT HUMMUS FOR WHICH I HAVE A QUICK-ROASTING TRICK. ONCE YOU'VE USED THESE RECIPES IT'LL BE EASY TO TRY OTHER VARIATIONS, SUCH AS ROASTED BEETROOT HUMMUS, HARISSA OR SUNDRIED TOMATO HUMMUS AND SPINACH AND FETA DIP.

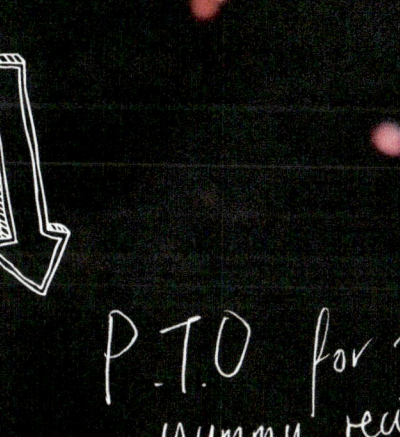

P.T.O for the yummy recipes

BABA GHANOUSH

PREPARATION TIME: 10 MIN
COOKING TIME: 10 MIN
SERVES 4

2 large aubergines, about 400g each
30ml tahini paste
juice of 1 lemon
1 clove garlic, crushed
2ml ground cumin
pinch of smoked sea salt
30ml sesame oil
30ml pomegranate rubies, to garnish
2ml cayenne pepper, to garnish
dash of olive oil

METHOD

Prick the aubergines a few times and push a skewer through each one, then char them on the outside by placing them directly on the flame of a gas ring. Turn them as the skin chars until they are uniformly charred on the outside. (If you don't have a gas stove, you can char them under the grill in your oven, remembering to turn them for even charring.)

Place on a microwave-safe plate and microwave for 5 minutes, or until soft. Transfer them to a resealable freezer bag for 5 minutes to allow them to sweat and cool down. (The sweating makes it easier to remove the charred skin.) When cool enough to handle, peel off the skin.

Cut each aubergine in half and use a teaspoon to scrape and remove all the seeds. In a food processor, blend the aubergine flesh with the rest of the ingredients to form a smooth paste. Transfer to a serving dish, garnish with pomegranate rubies, sprinkle with a bit of cayenne pepper and drizzle with olive oil before serving.

SCAN TO WATCH
A VIDEO ON
HOW TO
MAKE THIS RECIPE

Siba's tip...
If you're not so keen on the smoky flavour produced by grilling the skin of the aubergines, you can always cook them in a preheated oven at 180°C for 35 minutes and then continue in the usual way.

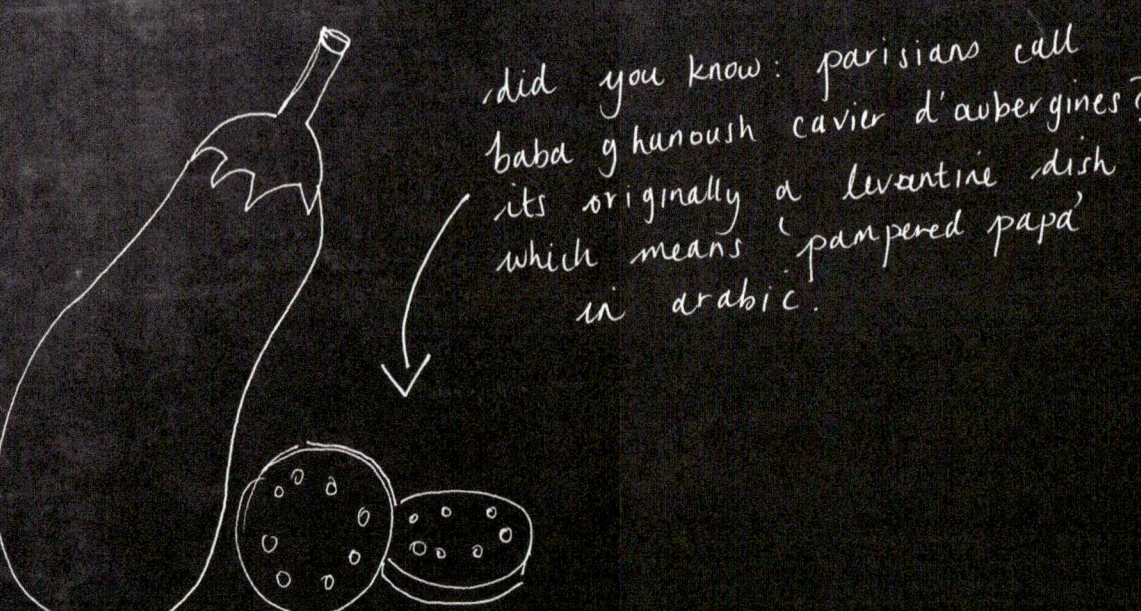

did you know: parisians call baba ghanoush cavier d'aubergines? its originally a levantine dish which means 'pampered papa' in arabic.

ROAST BUTTERNUT HUMMUS

PREPARATION TIME: 10 MIN
COOKING TIME: 40 MIN
SERVES 6

1 medium butternut, peeled,
seeded and cubed
1 clove garlic, banged to crush
with the peel
pinch of sea salt, to taste
3ml butter
15ml honey
125ml chickpeas, rinsed and
drained (optional)
30ml tahini paste
juice of 1 lemon
2ml ground cumin, toasted
30ml sesame oil
30ml extra virgin olive oil
dash of balsamic vinegar
pinch of black salt (optional)

METHOD

Preheat the oven to 180°C and lightly grease a baking tray with oil. Place the butternut and the garlic clove on the tray and season with sea salt. Dot with butter and drizzle with honey.

Roast for 40 minutes until golden and tender. Set aside to cool. Remove the peel from the garlic. Place the roasted butternut and garlic in a blender with the rest of the ingredients and process to a smooth paste. Transfer to a serving dish and drizzle with a dash of balsamic vinegar and black salt to garnish, if you're using it, just before serving.

Siba's tip...

To speed up the roasting time, you can microwave the butternut for 5 minutes until cooked and tender, place on the greased baking tray and season with salt, a dot of butter and a drizzle of honey before roasting it for 20 minutes until golden.

RED PEPPER HUMMUS

PREPARATION TIME: 10 MIN
COOKING TIME: 10 MIN
SERVES 4–6

2 red peppers, roasted
400g can chickpeas,
rinsed and drained
30ml tahini paste
juice of 1 lemon
1 clove garlic
2ml ground cumin
pinch of sea salt, to taste
3ml sesame oil
30ml extra virgin olive oil,
plus extra to drizzle
paprika, to garnish

METHOD

Cut the red peppers in half, remove the seeds and white pith and place on a greased baking tray with the skin-side up. Place under the grill in an oven preheated to 230°C and roast for about 10 minutes until tender and the top skin is charred. Transfer to a resealable freezer bag, allow the peppers to cool, then peel off the charred skin.

Tip the roasted red peppers into a blender along with the chickpeas and the rest of the ingredients, and process to a smooth paste. Transfer to a serving dish and drizzle with extra virgin olive oil before serving. Garnish with a dust of paprika.

SCAN TO WATCH
A VIDEO ON
HOW TO
MAKE THIS RECIPE

the fresher the better

HOMEMADE PESTO

THIS PESTO CAN BE MADE WITH FRESH BASIL OR WILD ROCKET LEAVES. IF YOU DON'T HAVE A BLENDER OR A PESTLE AND MORTAR, CHOP THE INGREDIENTS WITH A KNIFE, STARTING WITH THE HERBS, GARLIC AND OPTIONAL CHILI. THEN CHOP THE NUTS AND MIX EVERYTHING TO FORM A PASTE. ADD THE PARMESAN CHEESE AND STIR IN THE OIL.

PREPARATION TIME: 10 MIN
NO COOKING TIME
MAKES 250ml

200g fresh basil or wild rocket
2 cloves garlic, crushed
1 green chili, pith and
seeds removed (optional)
sea salt and freshly ground
black pepper
175ml pine nuts, toasted
235ml Parmesan cheese, grated
60ml olive oil

METHOD

If you're not making this pesto by hand, place all the ingredients, apart from the olive oil, in a food processor and blend until smooth.

Then add the olive oil and blend to thicken. Transfer to a sterilised jar and cover with a layer of oil to seal. Store in the fridge until needed.

Siba's tip...

To sterilise a jar, wash it along with its lid and rubber seal in hot soapy water and rinse. Place the jar, with its open side down, and the lid to dry on a baking tray in a preheated oven at 180°C for 20 minutes. Meanwhile, submerge and boil the rubber seal in water for the same amount of time. Remove the jar from the oven and fill it with the pesto, closing when it's cold or the same temperature as the pesto. You can freeze the pesto for up to 3 months by leaving out the cheese and placing it in a sterilised jar. Add the cheese once it has defrosted.

CAPE MALAY MARINADE + RELISH

I love this Cape Malay-inspired two-in-one recipe as it's both spicy and sweet and sour at once. The marinade works well with meat, chicken and fish while the relish is delicious with meat and pap (maize meal). My favourite is to use it for the South African dish of 'pap and vleis' by infusing the meat in the marinade and then serving it with pap and the relish.

METHOD

PREPARATION TIME: 10 MIN
COOKING TIME: 10 MIN
EACH MAKES 375ml

30ml oil
2 large onions, finely chopped
1 clove garlic, crushed
30ml Cape Malay spice mix
(see Siba's tip for recipe)
½ red chili, seeded and chopped
2 dried bay leaves
1 dried curry leaves (optional)
30ml apricot chutney
45ml apricot jam
250ml apple cider vinegar
2ml fresh ginger, grated
250ml milk

RELISH
410g can peeled and
chopped tomatoes
45ml smoky barbecue sauce
250g cherry tomatoes
salt, to taste

Heat the oil and sauté the onion and garlic for 2 minutes. Add the spice mix, chili, bay and curry leaves and stir for a minute.

Stir in the chutney and jam and then pour in the vinegar, taking care not to breathe in the heated vinegar as it'll cause you to sneeze.

Simmer over medium heat for 10 minutes and stir in the fresh ginger at the end. Transfer half the mixture to a jug and mix with the milk to make the marinade.

Add the can of chopped tomatoes, smoky barbecue sauce and cherry tomatoes to the remaining mixture in the pan. Simmer for 10 minutes until the flavours have fused and the cherry tomatoes are soft. Check whether further seasoning is required, and adjust if necessary. Serve as a relish with meat and pap.

Siba's tip...
To make the Cape Malay spice, mix 5ml coriander seeds with 2ml each of ground ginger, cinnamon, mustard seeds, fennel seeds, fenugreek and garlic flakes, and blend in an electric grinder or with a pestle and mortar until powdery. Add 5ml each of turmeric and cumin, a pinch of freshly ground black pepper and salt, and place in a sealable container. If you don't have apricot chutney you can use any of the usual chutneys on sale in your supermarket. If you don't have any chutney in your pantry, simply increase the amount of apricot jam by 30ml.

PEPPADEW DIP

I FIRST MADE THIS DIP YEARS AGO WHEN I COOKED FOR TWO OF SOUTH AFRICA'S POPULAR SOCCER STARS AND SERVED IT WITH GRILLED CHICKEN WINGS. IT CAN ALSO BE USED IN PLACE OF TARTAR SAUCE WITH FRIED OR GRILLED FISH OR WITH CORN CHIPS AND VEGGIE CRUDITÉS.

PREPARATION TIME: 15 MIN
NO COOKING TIME
SERVES 6

125ml mayonnaise
60ml crème fraîche (optional)
8 jarred peppadews, drained
and chopped
15ml coriander, rinsed
and chopped
5ml freshly ground red
peppercorns
juice of ½ or 1 lime

METHOD

Mix the dip ingredients together until well combined.

Serve with a handful each of baby carrots, halved or quartered lengthways, and halved celery sticks. Cucumber sticks, halved radishes, raw butternut or pumpkin sticks and asparagus tips also taste good with it.

SCAN TO WATCH
A VIDEO ON
HOW TO
MAKE THIS RECIPE

Siba's tip...
The crème fraîche makes the dip thicker and gives it a creamy texture. I used tangy mayonnaise, but if you can't find that then regular mayonnaise is fine.

TZATZIKI

THIS GREEK SAUCE, WHICH I ALSO SERVE AS A DIP, IS A STANDARD AND USUAL COMPANION FOR MY MEATBALL PITAS THAT WE OFTEN TAKE ON PICNICS. BE SURE TO STORE THE TZATZIKI IN A SEALED CONTAINER SO IT DOESN'T SPILL IN THE PICNIC BASKET.

PREPARATION TIME: 10 MIN
NO COOKING TIME
SERVES 4-6

½ cucumber
125ml Bulgarian or
Greek yoghurt
30ml sour cream (optional)
1 clove garlic, crushed
5ml fresh mint, finely chopped
sea salt and freshly ground
black pepper, to taste

SERVE WITH
6 thin slices of ciabatta
1 clove garlic, to rub
15ml olive oil, to drizzle

METHOD

Slice the cucumber in half and scrape out the seeds with a spoon, then grate it and squeeze out any excess moisture before transferring to a bowl.

Add the rest of the ingredients and stir to combine. Season with salt and pepper to taste.

Brush the sliced ciabattas with garlic and drizzle them with oil before grilling in a preheated oven at 200°C for about 5 minutes on each side, or until crisp and golden.

Siba's tip...
To give the tzatziki a thicker consistency, you can strain the yoghurt using a muslin cloth placed in a colander over a bowl for 2 hours. You can also add 5ml each of dill and parsley, and the juice of a lemon wedge, for a bit of a kick.

Jazz up the colour when serving with a few red pepper corns, olive oil and mint or red dill leaves. Yum!

When I'm in the Kitchen

I LOVE TO

SPICE THINGS UP

BALSAMIC VINEGAR DRESSING

180ml extra virgin olive oil
60ml balsamic vinegar
5ml Dijon mustard
5ml onion, very finely chopped
or grated
1 small clove garlic,
finely crushed
2ml honey, to taste
sea salt and freshly ground
black pepper, to taste

THIS DRESSING NEEDS ONLY FOUR INGREDIENTS: EXTRA VIRGIN OLIVE OIL, BALSAMIC VINEGAR AND SALT AND PEPPER TO SEASON, BUT I LIKE ADDING 5ML OF DIJON MUSTARD WITH THE SAME AMOUNT OF VERY FINELY GRATED ONION TO GIVE IT EXTRA PUNCH. IT'S PARTICULARLY DELICIOUS ON POACHED EGGS AND SIMPLE SALADS.

METHOD

In a jug, mix together all the ingredients and whisk until well combined.

Siba's tip...

The solid parts will sink to the bottom after a little while and the oil and vinegar will separate, so it's important to give it a good stir before using. Keep the dressing chilled and covered in a sterilised jar.

COCONUT DRESSING

PREPARATION TIME: 5 MIN
NO COOKING TIME
MAKES 125ml

25ml soy sauce
15ml sesame oil
25ml rice wine vinegar
1 long spring onion, finely chopped
7ml fresh ginger, grated
30ml coriander, finely chopped
1 clove garlic, crushed
80ml coconut cream
2ml (7 drops) Tabasco sauce
pinch of sugar, to taste

THIS IS A PUNGENT DRESSING THAT WORKS WELL WITH THE ASIAN RIBBON SALAD ON PAGE 71. IT ALSO GOES WELL WITH MOST RAW SALADS, AS LONG AS YOU LIKE THE TASTE AND TEXTURE OF COCONUT CREAM.

METHOD

Mix the dressing ingredients in a jar or jug and shake or whisk well. Drizzle over the salad just before serving.

Siba's tip...

If this dressing is chilled, the cream will harden so be sure to take it out of the fridge early enough to reach room temperature, and become liquid again, before serving.

RANCH DRESSING

PREPARATION TIME: 10 MIN
NO COOKING TIME
MAKES ABOUT 300ml

125ml mayonnaise
125ml buttermilk or amasi
125ml sour cream
15ml fresh lemon juice
5ml Dijon mustard
30ml onion, very finely chopped
1 clove garlic, crushed
15ml fresh parsley, chopped
15ml fresh chives, chopped
pinch of salt and freshly ground black pepper, to taste

THIS IS A VERSATILE SALAD DRESSING AND THE ULTIMATE SAUCE FOR BURGERS. I SOMETIMES USE IT INSTEAD OF TZATZIKI WITH MY MEATBALL PITAS AND EVEN WITH FISH AND CHIPS AS AN ALTERNATIVE TO TARTAR SAUCE.

METHOD

Mix all the dressing ingredients together and stir well to combine.

Siba's tip...

This dressing is best served chilled, and goes very well with the red kidney + avo salad on page 81 and the cobb salad burger on page 113. You can add 5ml of pickled chopped jalapeños for a slightly pickled taste and some heat.

SPICY CORN RUB

THIS SPICY RUB IDEA ORIGINATES FROM MY EXPERIENCE OF THE STREET-FOOD CULTURE IN KENYA, WHERE THEY BRAAI FRESH CORN, COVER IT IN A RED SPICY RUB AND THEN WRAP IT IN NEWSPAPER. IT WAS SO GOOD THAT I HAD TO CREATE MY OWN MIX INSPIRED BY IT.

PREPARATION TIME: 5 MIN
COOKING TIME: 10 MIN
SERVES 6

SPICE MIX
30ml smoked salt
15ml cayenne pepper
30ml chili flakes
30ml dried mixed herbs
30ml smoked paprika
2ml lime zest (optional)

SERVE WITH
6 fresh corn cobs
30ml butter

METHOD

Combine the spice mix ingredients and place aside. Soak the corn cobs in a bowl of cold water until ready to cook – this will prevent them from burning and popping while braaing.

Braai the corn cobs for 10 minutes or so until cooked, making sure you turn them every few minutes. Once cooked and charred remove from the grill. Brush with butter and sprinkle generously with the spice mix.

Siba's tip...
Keep the spice mix in a sterilised jar. Just make sure the jar is completely dry before putting it in. To use as a meat rub, add a little olive oil to make it easier to brush over the meat before braaing.

SMOKY TOMATO RELISH

THIS SPICY RELISH CAN BE SERVED WARM OR COLD AND GOES WELL WITH BRAAIED FISH AND MEAT. IT ALSO KEEPS WELL IN THE FRIDGE AND IS A WINNER ON GOURMET SANDWICHES OR WARMED UP WITH CHICKEN OR PASTA.

PREPARATION TIME: 10 MIN
COOKING TIME: 30 MIN
SERVES 6

30ml olive oil
1 onion, finely chopped
1 green pepper, cored and diced
2 cloves garlic, crushed
5cm fresh ginger, finely chopped or grated
70g chorizo sausage, diced
1 large aubergine (400g), sprinkled with salt, wiped and finely chopped
30ml smoked paprika
10ml tomato paste
400g can peeled and chopped tomatoes
375ml chicken stock
sea salt and freshly ground black pepper, to taste
1 baguette, cut into slices and toasted (optional)

METHOD

Heat the oil in a large saucepan and sauté the onion and green pepper for 3 minutes. Add the garlic and ginger and stir for a minute. Add the chorizo, aubergine and paprika and sauté over a high heat for 4 minutes.

Lower the heat to medium and cook for about 3 minutes until the aubergine is soft. Add the tomato paste and stir well. Add the canned tomatoes and cook for 2 minutes while stirring. Pour in the stock, bring to the boil and simmer, half-covered, for about 10 minutes until thickened. Season if necessary.

Serve immediately with the toasted baguette slices, or pour into a sterilised jar and refrigerate until needed.

SCAN TO WATCH
A VIDEO ON
HOW TO
MAKE THIS RECIPE

Siba's tip...
When sautéing the chorizo, allow it to release some of its red spicy oil, but not too much, otherwise it'll become too dry. It's a great relish for my surf + turf braai on page 109.

Try mixing this fabulous relish into a plate of penne - it gives your taste buds a rare treat!

HARISSA CIABATTA

FIERY HARISSA PASTE MAKES A FREQUENT APPEARANCE IN MY KITCHEN. I PREFER TO MAKE IT MYSELF TO GIVE MEATS, SAUCES AND SALAD DRESSINGS A BIT OF SPICY HEAT, OR SIMPLY A TASTE OF NORTH AFRICA.

PREPARATION TIME: 15 MIN
COOKING TIME: 5 MIN
SERVES 4-6

HARISSA PASTE
3 red chilies, seeds and pith removed
1 red pepper, roasted and
skin removed
6 cloves garlic, roughly chopped
30ml ginger, roughly sliced
pinch of salt
5ml ground cumin
5ml ground coriander
15ml fresh coriander, rinsed
and drained
4 sprigs fresh thyme leaves
30ml olive oil

HARISSA CIABATTA
200ml unsalted butter, softened
1 large ciabatta loaf, sliced
in half horizontally
1 ball buffalo mozzarella
10ml parsley, roughly chopped
10ml chives, roughly chopped

METHOD

Place all the harissa paste ingredients, apart from the oil, in a food processor, and blend to a thick paste.

Add the oil while still blending until well combined, lighter in colour and paste-like. Use immediately or store in a sterilised jar with a layer of oil on top to seal.

Mix the harissa paste with the softened butter and stir well to make harissa butter. Spread over both sides of the ciabatta, reserving the rest in the fridge.

Tear the mozzarella and place it on the bread. Grill in the oven at 220°C for 5 minutes, until the cheese has melted. Remove from the oven, slice and transfer to a serving board before sprinkling with the herbs. Serve open or as a sandwich.

SCAN TO WATCH
A VIDEO ON
HOW TO
MAKE THIS RECIPE

Siba's tip...
You can keep leftover harissa butter by rolling it into a log, wrapping it in plastic wrap and refrigerating or freezing it. Onions and garlic are great sautéd in it.

DRINKS

&

COCKTAILS

It's time to join me for refreshing and scintillating
jewel-coloured drinks. Viva!

THESE TWO DRINKS ARE THE BOMB! SERIOUSLY, THEY'RE ABSOLUTELY DELECTABLE AND A MUST AS SUMMER TREATS, BOTH FOR YOU AND YOUR SPECIAL GUESTS.

GINGER + ROOIBOS INFUSED BERRY SORBET SLUSH

I FIRST USED THIS RECIPE AS A BERRY SORBET FOR MY CHRISTMAS SPECIAL MENU IN LONDON 2014. I LOVE SORBETS AND WANTED TO INFUSE ONE WITH ONE OF MY FAVOURITE INGREDIENTS, FRESH GINGER. I ALSO WANTED TO ADD A TYPICAL SOUTH AFRICAN INGREDIENT TO CELEBRATE MY ROOTS. ROOIBOS TEA WAS A PERFECT CHOICE AS THE COMBINATION WORKED VERY WELL. HERE, I SERVE IT AS A SLUSH INSTEAD OF A SORBET AND IT'S EQUALLY GOOD.

PREPARATION TIME: 15 MIN
COOKING TIME: 10 MIN
SERVES 4

SYRUP
400ml freshly squeezed orange juice
40ml fresh ginger, peeled and sliced
250ml caster sugar
1 rooibos teabag
1kg strawberries, washed and stalks removed
300g blueberries, washed
30ml lemon juice

GARNISH
50g blueberries
4 short wooden skewers

METHOD

Heat the orange juice in a saucepan with 10ml ginger and caster sugar for 10 minutes to make a light syrup. Remove from the heat, add the teabag and steep the teabag until the syrup has cooled.

Once cooled, remove the teabag and ginger and chill for 30 minutes. In a food processor, blend the strawberries and blueberries with the lemon juice and remaining 30ml ginger until almost smooth, but allowing some of the berry flesh to remain whole to add texture.

Pour into a jug and mix with the chilled ginger-infused syrup, stirring until combined. Pour into an ice cream machine and churn until thick. Divide into 4 glasses and serve each with 4 blueberries on a wooden skewer.

Siba's tip...

It takes much longer to make this without an ice cream machine, so it's a good idea to make it the day before you need it. After mixing the berry pulp with the syrup, pour into a metal container and freeze for 3-4 hours until rock solid frozen. Remove from the freezer, break into pieces and place in a processor to blend until smooth – this helps to remove the ice crystals and give the slush a smooth texture. Transfer back to the metal container and freeze again for an hour. Blend again and freeze until ready to use. For a quicker berry slush, mix the syrup and berry pulp with the ice and blend.

GRANADILLA, COCONUT + CHILI DREAM

THE GRANADILLA, COCONUT AND CHILI DREAM CAME ABOUT SIMPLY WHILE DAYDREAMING OF MAKING A BEVERAGE COMBINING THOSE INGREDIENTS. I HAD A CERTAIN TASTE IN MIND AND WHEN I EVENTUALLY HAD THE CHANCE TO CREATE IT, IT WAS EXACTLY WHAT I'D BEEN HOPING FOR. IT'S A DEFINITE HOME FAVOURITE.

PREPARATION TIME: 5 MIN
COOKING TIME: 15 MIN
SERVES 4

SUGAR SYRUP
125ml water
125ml sugar

8 granadillas (passion fruits)
2 pineapples, cored and
cut into pieces
500ml ice, crushed
500ml granadilla sorbet
125ml coconut cream
250ml passion fruit juice
1 red chili, cored and seeded

GARNISH
pineapple slices, quartered
mint leaves
2 red chilies, halved
4 short wooden skewers

METHOD

Place 125ml water and 125ml sugar into a saucepan and heat, stirring to dissolve the sugar. Allow to boil over medium heat for about 10-15 minutes until syrupy. Allow to cool in the fridge for at least 15 minutes.

In a food processor, blend the granadilla pulp and pineapple until smooth. Add the crushed ice, sorbet and coconut cream and blend again.

Mix 30ml of the cooled syrup and blended fruit mixture with the fruit juice, add the chili and stir. Pour into glasses and serve, garnishing each with a piece of pineapple, a sprig of mint and half a red chili on a skewer.

Siba's tip...
If you're serving cocktails, this is fabulous with 60ml of rum.
The flavours absolutely complement each other.

GREEN LEMONADE FLOATS

I CAN'T RESIST HAVING A FRESH JUICE WHEN I VISIT A MARKET. IF IT'S NOT KALE OR SPINACH WITH A SHOT OF GINGER, THEN IT'S SURE TO BE A BEETROOT MIX. I LOVE THEM SO MUCH THAT I ALSO MAKE THEM AT HOME, WITH A 'SIBALICIOUS TWIST' OF COURSE. SPINACH AND KALE JUICE HAS A VERY EARTHY FLAVOUR SO I LIGHTEN IT UP WITH GREEN APPLES, CELERY, CUCUMBER, A SHOT OF LIME, GINGER AND CRUSHED ICE. BUT WHAT REALLY MAKES THIS RECIPE SPECIAL IS THE LIME SORBET THAT FLOATS ON TOP — THE COLD SOUR CITRUS TASTE OF THE LIME WITH THE HEALTHY GREEN MIXTURE IS JUST INCREDIBLE.

PREPARATION TIME: 10 MIN
NO COOKING TIME
SERVES 4

250ml spinach or kale,
thoroughly washed
6 green apples
2 celery sticks
½ cucumber
5cm piece fresh ginger
juice of ½ lime

SERVE WITH
500ml ice, crushed
8 scoops of lime sorbet

METHOD

In a juicer, juice all the solid ingredients, pour into a jug, and mix with the lime juice and finely crushed ice.

Pour into glasses, top each with 2 scoops of lime sorbet and serve straight away.

Siba's tip...
For a slightly different taste, use red apples instead of green and a bit of pineapple juice or a mixture of both. Freshly squeezed juices are best served chilled with crushed ice rather than at room temperature. They can be bottled and kept in the fridge for 2-3 days as long as the lime has been added as it acts as a preservative.

SIBA'S SUNDOWNER

I FIRST MADE THIS COCKTAIL WHEN I HAD MY GIRLFRIENDS OVER FOR A GIRLS' GET TOGETHER. I WANTED SOMETHING DIFFERENT, TASTY AND QUICK TO PREPARE, SO, I USED A VARIATION OF STORE-BOUGHT JUICES, ADDED A SHOT OF VODKA TO THE GLASSES AND GARNISHED THEM WITH CELERY LEAVES AND ORANGES SLICES. IT WAS DELICIOUS! IT'S EQUALLY REFRESHING AS A VIRGIN COCKTAIL, WITHOUT THE VODKA.

PREPARATION TIME: 10 MIN
NO COOKING TIME
SERVES 4

300ml pomegranate juice
300ml apple juice
300ml orange juice
300ml carrot juice
¼ celery stick, finely grated
20ml fresh ginger,
grated or juiced

MIX + SERVE WITH
250ml ice, crushed
60ml vodka (optional)
2 oranges, sliced
6–8 sprigs of celery leaves
a few mint leaves (optional)

METHOD

Place all the juice ingredients into a jug and mix well to combine. Add the finely grated celery stick and ginger. Place the crushed ice into 4 glasses and pour a shot of vodka into each.

Fold and concertina each orange slice to make a zig-zag shape and secure with a toothpick. Place one in each glass along with a sprig of celery leaves.

Top with mint leaves, pour in the juice and serve immediately.

Siba's tip...

You can also fold each orange slice using a celery stick as a skewer and place in the glass with the mint leaves.

I always think of
vegetable and
fruit drinks as
the elixir of life.

FRUITY ROOIBOS SUMMER BLUSH

THIS IS A GREAT SUMMER DRINK FOR CHILDREN. I ALWAYS MAKE IT WHEN I HAVE LOTS OF KIDS AROUND AS IT'S EASY TO REFILL AND GOES A LONG WAY — I JUST MAKE SURE I HAVE MORE THAN ENOUGH CHILLED ROOIBOS TEA TO KEEP TOPPING UP THE JUGS. IT'S A HEALTHY ALTERNATIVE TO ALL THE CARBONATED AND SUGARY SOFT DRINKS OUT THERE AND VERY REFRESHING FOR ADULTS TOO.

PREPARATION TIME: 10 MIN
NO COOKING TIME
SERVES 6-8

1,5 litres rooibos tea
60ml honey
500ml ice, crushed
2 lemons, sliced and
pips removed
250g strawberries, halved
or sliced
125ml fresh cherries, halved
and pitted
125ml pomegranate rubies

METHOD

To make the tea, place 3 rooibos tea bags and the honey in a large jug and pour in 1,5 litres of boiling water. Stir and allow to cool to room temperature. Cover and place in the fridge until chilled and ready to use.

Place the crushed ice in 1 or 2 large jugs and add the lemons, strawberries, cherries and pomegranate rubies. Pour in the chilled rooibos tea and serve immediately.

Siba's tip...
You can vary the sweetness by adding more or less honey Store-bought iced rooibos tea also works, as do the sparkling variations.

" **NAMES LIKE** SINGAPOR

HAWAII, CUBA LIBRE, PIÑA

BREEZE AND MANHATTAN AU

OF YESTERYEAR'S CHIC PART

BUT, WE LIVE IN A MORE HEA

I'VE COME UP WITH A FEW R

YOU TO TRY. CHEERS, OR AS

SLING, BAHAMA MAMA, BLUE
COLADA, COSMOPOLITAN, SEA
OMATICALLY MAKE ME THINK
S IN NEW YORK AND PARIS.
TH-CONSCIOUS ERA NOW, SO
RESHING ALTERNATIVES FOR
WE SAY AT HOME, IMPILO!"

SIBA'S SUNDAY SUNSHINE

THIS REALLY IS MY SUNDAY SPECIAL. I ALWAYS USE FRESH PINEAPPLES AND GINGER FROM OUR LOCAL MARKET AND JUICE THEM AT HOME. IT TASTES SO CRISP AND REFRESHING AND THE CARBONATED LEMONADE WITH THE KICK OF GINGER GIVES ONE A NEW ZEST FOR LIFE.

PREPARATION TIME: 10 MIN
NO COOKING TIME
SERVES 6

10 large pineapples, juiced
(to make 1 litre)
1 large piece fresh ginger, juiced
(to make 60ml)
1 litre carbonated lemonade,
chilled
juice of 1 lemon
250ml ice, crushed

GARNISH
4 kiwi fruits, peeled and sliced
60ml mint leaves, stems
attached (optional)
200g small strawberries,
quartered (if big then sliced)

METHOD

Juice the pineapple and ginger in a machine and mix with the lemonade and lemon juice in a large jar and stir well.

Place the crushed ice and kiwi fruit slices in small glasses. Top with the juice and garnish with mint and strawberries. Serve immediately.

Siba's tip...

Store-bought pineapple juice just isn't as good as freshly squeezed – a juicer is definitely a worthy investment. You can skim off the foam that forms while juicing the pineapple juice, but it's not essential as it'll taste good with and without it.

VIRGIN POMEGRANATE MOJITO

I FIRST MADE THIS MOJITO FOR A SPECIAL DATE NIGHT AT HOME WITH BRIAN. IT'S FRESH AND PRETTY AND THE POMEGRANATE RUBIES AND RASPBERRIES GIVE IT A FESTIVE TOUCH, SO IT'S GREAT TO SERVE WHEN YOU'RE HAVING SPECIAL GUESTS OVER.

PREPARATION TIME: 10 MIN
NO COOKING TIME
SERVES 6

600g raspberries
about 30 mint leaves
6 limes, cut into slices
30 ice blocks, crushed
500ml pomegranate
juice, chilled
500ml lemonade, chilled

METHOD

Place the raspberries, mint and lime slices in 6 glasses. Using a wooden spoon or muddler, partly crush some of the fruit and mint to release the juice and oils.

Add the crushed ice, fill with cold pomegranate juice and lemonade, and serve immediately.

Siba's tip...
You can refill the same glasses with the extra pomegranate juice and lemonade.

=193

SOMETHING...

sweet

I don't think it's a coincidence that stressed spelled backwards is desserts!

LIME CHEESECAKE

I LOVE CHEESECAKES. THIS ONE IS SUPER EASY TO MAKE AND USES JUST A HANDFUL OF INGREDIENTS. ALL YOU NEED IS ENOUGH TIME FOR IT TO SET SO BE SURE TO MAKE IT WELL IN ADVANCE. I OFTEN SERVE IT WHEN I'M HOSTING A FAMILY OR A GROUP OF FRIENDS AS I CAN MAKE IT THE DAY BEFORE I NEED IT, ADDING THE GARNISH JUST BEFORE SERVING. THIS WAY I DON'T NEED TO PREPARE ALL THREE COURSES ON THE SAME DAY AND HAVE MORE TIME TO SPEND WITH MY GUESTS. AS A HOST YOU DON'T WANT TO MISS OUT ON ALL THE FUN AND GOOD CONVERSATION!

PREPARATION TIME: 10 MIN
COOKING TIME: 5 MIN
CHILLING TIME: 12-24 HRS
SERVES 8

200ml butter
400g digestive biscuits

FILLING
2 x 250g tubs plain cream cheese
2 x 385g cans condensed milk
250ml fresh cream, whipped
juice and zest of 4 limes

GARNISH
125ml raspberries
30ml icing sugar, to dust

METHOD

Melt the butter in a saucepan and remove from the heat. Place the biscuits in a food processor and blend until they resemble fine crumbs. Add the crumbs to the melted butter and stir to combine. Tip into a greased and lined 28cm tin and press down with the back of a spoon.

Put the cream cheese in a bowl and whisk until soft and creamy. This will prevent lumps from forming and make it easier to combine with the other ingredients. Add the condensed milk and whisk again until well combined and smooth.

Stir in the lime juice and zest, reserving some of the zest to decorate. Whip the cream to soft peaks, then fold into the cream cheese and condensed milk mixture. Pour over the base and smooth over with the back of a spoon.

Place in the fridge and leave to set for at least 12 hours or up to a day. When set, remove from the tin and transfer to a serving plate or cake stand. Garnish with the raspberries, remaining zest and a sprinkle of icing sugar just before serving.

Siba's tip...
When making the biscuit base, try not to compress it too much as it'll then solidify and the cheesecake will be difficult to cut into slices. If you're using a 28cm tin, as suggested, then the cheesecake should set overnight, but if you're using a smaller tin, such as a 20, 22 or 23cm, it'll take longer to set. To make sure this dessert sets well you need to place it in the coldest section of the fridge, which is usually the lowest part just above the vegetable section of a standard modern fridge. Opening the fridge frequently will delay the setting process, so will a fridge that is full. If this is the case, put your fridge setting on the coldest option.

SCAN TO WATCH
A VIDEO ON
HOW TO
MAKE THIS RECIPE

FAMOUS TRIFLE

ON THOSE VERY FESTIVE OCCASIONS THAT WE USED TO HAVE AT HOME, LIKE CHRISTMAS, EASTER OR A BIRTHDAY CELEBRATION, JELLY TRIFLE WAS SURE TO BE THE MAIN DESSERT OF THE DAY. IT WAS ALWAYS MY JOB TO MAKE THE DIFFERENT JELLY LAYERS IN A RAINBOW-LIKE PATTERN. I LOVED THE TRIFLE BUT HATED MY JOB AS IT WAS SUCH A BORING AND TEDIOUS PROCESS. THAT'S WHY THIS IS A JELLY-LESS TRIFLE! IT TASTES AND LOOKS ABSOLUTELY STUNNING AND YOU CAN EAT IT AS SOON AS YOU'VE MADE IT. I COULDN'T BE HAPPIER.

PREPARATION TIME: 20 MIN
COOKING TIME: 10 MIN
SERVES 8

BERRY SAUCE
400g mixed frozen berries
zest of 1 lemon
250ml caster sugar
60ml water

LAYERING
500g (2 tubs) plain cream cheese, at room temperature
1 litre strawberry yoghurt
4 mini Swiss rolls or 1 large, cut into thin slices
1 or 1,5 litres good quality ready-made custard
250g fresh raspberries
250g fresh strawberries, quartered
100g blueberries
125g gooseberries (optional)
125ml cream, whipped (optional)
80g fresh cherries (optional)

METHOD

Place the frozen berries in a medium-sized saucepan and heat for a few minutes until they soften, then crush them with a fork. Add the lemon zest, sugar and water, and cook for 5 minutes until the mixture has thickened and reduced. Set aside to cool completely.

Whisk the cream cheese until soft and smooth and place it in a large dish. Add the fruit yoghurt a little at a time, beating well after each addition to prevent any lumps from forming. Continue until all the yoghurt has been combined with the cream cheese.

In a deep glass trifle dish, arrange the mini Swiss roll slices up the sides and on the base. Top with the custard and yoghurt and cream cheese mix. Drizzle the cooled berry sauce around the edge, followed by a layer of the fresh berries.

Repeat the layering with the Swiss roll, custard, yoghurt and cream cheese mix, berry sauce and fresh mixed berries, until the dish is filled. Top with cream and more berries.

Garnish with the cherries and serve immediately or cover with plastic wrap and keep in the fridge until you need it.

SCAN TO WATCH
A VIDEO ON
HOW TO
MAKE THIS RECIPE

Siba's tip...
The great thing about this trifle is that you can use a variety of fruits, either seasonal or those you like most. It's best to chill it for 20 minutes before serving, but it's also fine served immediately. Trifle is one of those desserts you have to dish at the table so it can take centre stage while it looks beautiful. Once served, it doesn't look as good!

TROPICAL PAVLOVA

THIS IS SUCH A DELIGHTFUL DESSERT AND RELATIVELY EASY TO MAKE BECAUSE ALL YOU NEED TO BAKE IS THE MERINGUE BASE. MY INSPIRATION FOR IT CAME FROM THE FLAVOURS OF AN ETON MESS. HOWEVER, I WANTED A MORE DRAMATIC VERSION OF IT AND ONE I COULD SERVE AS A CENTREPIECE, RATHER THAN INDIVIDUAL SERVINGS. THIS WAS THE FABULOUS RESULT.

PREPARATION TIME: 20 MIN
BAKING TIME: 1.5 HRS
SERVES 8

6 egg whites
2ml cream of tartar
500ml caster sugar
a few drops of pink or red colouring (optional)

FILLING
2 x 250g tubs plain cream cheese, room temperature
60ml caster sugar
juice of 1 lemon
5ml vanilla extract
250ml cream, whipped

SERVE WITH
2-4 mangoes, peeled and cubed
500ml mango sorbet
500ml passion fruit sorbet
50g pistachio nuts, chopped
8 granadillas, pulp scooped out
a few mint leaves, to garnish

SCAN TO WATCH
A VIDEO ON
HOW TO
MAKE THIS RECIPE

METHOD

Preheat the oven to 120°C and lightly grease and line a large baking sheet with baking paper. Trace the outline of a dinner plate in the middle of the baking paper, about 25cm in diameter. In a large clean glass bowl, beat the egg whites with an electric beater, until frothy, and add the cream of tartar, beating until soft peaks form.

Add 30ml of sugar at a time, beating after each addition until all the sugar has been used and the mixture is thick and glossy with firm white peaks. This takes about 10 minutes or so. Stir in a few drops of colouring, if using.

Transfer the meringue to the baking sheet using a spatula and spread it, using the marked circle as a guide. Create a bit of a well or indent in the centre for the filling. Bake in the oven for between 1 hour 20 minutes and 1 hour 30 minutes, until crispy on the outside but still soft inside. Allow to cool down completely.

Meanwhile, whisk the cream cheese, sugar and lemon juice until combined. Stir in the vanilla extract and fold in the cream.

Once the meringue has cooled down completely, assemble the pavlova by placing the meringue on a serving platter and topping it with the cream cheese mixture, mango, sorbet scoops, pistachio nuts and granadilla pulp. Garnish with the mint leaves and serve immediately.

Siba's tip...
When separating the eggs, make sure there isn't even a drop of egg yolk or fat in the egg white, as that will prevent it from fluffing up when whisked. Also be sure to use a squeaky clean glass bowl. Meringues are best cooked at low temperature for a long period of time so they can become crispy on the outside without browning.

PISTACHIO + CRANBERRY COOKIES

These cookies are so delicious that they disappear one by one as I take them out of the oven. Lasting two or three days would be a record! So, to control the number of biscuits eaten, I make a big batch of mixture and bake only one roll at a time. I then freeze the other rolls, and when I need one, leave it out to thaw, cut it into slices and pop them in the oven. It's an old recipe that I keep reinventing. Once I served them with ice cream and passion fruit sauce for a date night at home with Brian, which he really enjoyed.

PREPARATION TIME: 25 MIN
COOKING TIME: 15 MIN
MAKES 36–45 COOKIES

4 x 250ml all-purpose flour
pinch of salt
350ml unsalted butter, cut into pieces
250ml caster sugar
30–60ml cold water
125ml dried cranberries, roughly chopped
115ml pistachio nuts, roughly chopped

SAUCE
5 passion fruits, halved
80ml shop-bought passion fruit juice
15ml caster sugar

SERVE WITH
scoops of vanilla ice cream
60ml pistachio nuts, chopped
10ml dried cranberries, roughly chopped
15ml icing sugar (optional)

METHOD

Preheat the oven to 180°C and lightly grease and line a baking tray with baking paper. You'll need more baking trays if you're baking all the biscuits at once. Place the flour and salt in a large mixing bowl.

Add the butter and rub with your fingers until it resembles breadcrumbs. Add the sugar and work it until a dough is formed, using a sprinkle of cold water, if needed, to combine. Mix in the cranberries and pistachio nuts.

Divide into three, roll into thick logs and either cover two with cling wrap and freeze until you need them, or cut all three into 12–15 slices. Place on the baking trays and bake for 12–15 minutes until slightly golden. Remove from the oven and allow to cool slightly before transferring to a wire rack to cool completely.

In the meantime, scoop out the pulp and seeds from the passion fruits (granadillas) and add to a food processor with the juice and sugar. Whizz for a minute, until blended. Pass through muslin into a jug and chill until needed.

Serve 4–6 biscuits with a scoop of vanilla ice cream on each dessert plate. Top with the chopped nuts and cranberries, drizzle with the passion fruit sauce and dust with the icing sugar.

Siba's tip...
When rolling the dough into logs, makes sure you compress it well so that it's compact enough to make slices without holes. If you've frozen a batch, make sure to thaw the roll properly before slicing and baking it. Leave space in between each slice on the baking tray to allow room for expansion, otherwise they'll stick together and lose their shape.

COCONUT MACAROONS

THESE DAINTY TREATS ARE A FAVOURITE WHEN I WANT TO MAKE BITE-SIZED DESSERTS INSTEAD OF ONE BIG DESSERT. I CHOP AND CHANGE THE FILLING AND HAVE TRIED STRAWBERRY JAM, GRANADILLA COULIS, MELTED HAZELNUT CHOCOLATE SPREAD AND NOW GUAVA PRESERVE. THEY'RE OFTEN CONFUSED WITH THE FRENCH MACARONS (ONE 'O' INSTEAD OF TWO) AND ALTHOUGH THEY USE SIMILAR INGREDIENTS, THEY'RE WORLDS APART. THESE ARE VERY EASY TO MAKE COMPARED TO THEIR FRENCH COUSINS.

PREPARATION TIME: 15 MIN
BAKING TIME: 12–15 MIN
SERVES 6 OR MORE

2 large egg whites
pinch of cream of tartar
pinch of salt
60ml caster sugar
250ml desiccated coconut
100ml ground almonds
80ml guava preserve or jam
30ml icing sugar

METHOD

Preheat the oven to 180°C and lightly grease a baking tray with butter. Whisk the egg whites until frothy, then add the cream of tartar and salt. Continue whisking until soft peaks form, then add the sugar, a little at a time, until thick, stiff and glossy peaks form.

Fold in the coconut and ground almonds. Scoop 2 tablespoonfuls into your hands at a time and gently shape into balls. Be careful not to squeeze out the air that was incorporated by the whisking. Then make a small indentation in the centre of each one with your forefinger.

Place on a baking tray and bake for 8–10 minutes until puffed and slightly golden. Remove from the oven, and place on a wire rack to cool. Spoon the guava preserve filling into the macaroons and lightly dust with icing sugar just before serving.

SOMETHING SWEET

Siba's tip...
If some macaroons crack a bit while baking, just push the sides up while still warm to create a more pronounced indentation and shape.

GIANT CHOC CHIP COOKIES

IT SEEMS THAT OUR SON LONWABO HAS HIS DADDY'S SWEET TOOTH. HE LOVES THESE GIANT CHOC CHIP COOKIES, AND I ALWAYS GET A KISS AND AN 'I LOVE YOU MAMA' WHEN WE BAKE THEM, ESPECIALLY IF WE'VE MADE THEM TOGETHER. THAT'S WHY I CALL THEM PRECIOUS LONWABO'S TREATS.

PREPARATION TIME: 10 MIN
BAKING TIME: 15 MIN
MAKES 15

250ml butter, cubed
300ml caster sugar
4 large eggs
550ml plain flour, sifted
5ml vanilla extract
250ml dark chocolate chips

METHOD

Preheat the oven to 180°C and lightly grease a baking tray with butter and line with baking paper. Place the butter in a large mixing bowl and use an electric beater to cream the butter and sugar together, until light and fluffy.

Add the eggs, one at a time, beating well after each addition, until smooth and all the eggs have been incorporated. You may need to add a little flour between adding the eggs to prevent the mixture from separating.

Add the vanilla extract and gently fold the remaining flour into the creamed mixture. Add the chocolate chips and gently stir to combine. Scoop large teaspoonfuls of the mixture and place on the prepared baking tray. Lightly flatten with a fork.

Bake for 15 minutes until golden. Once cooked, transfer onto a cooling rack to cool completely. Serve with milk and place the rest in an airtight container.

Siba's tip...

You could make smaller cookies by scooping out a ½ teaspoonful of the mixture instead of large teaspoonfuls, and reducing the baking time to 8-10 minutes. Since the cookie mixture freezes well, you can place the raw cookies on a baking tray, cover with plastic wrap and freeze. Then bake them straight from frozen for about 12 minutes.

I love peanut butter !!

PEANUT BUTTER BANANA SANDWICH

I SIMPLY ADORE THIS OPEN SANDWICH AND HAVE RECENTLY DISCOVERED THAT A SCOOP OF VANILLA ICE CREAM TAKES IT TO THE NEXT LEVEL. IT'S MY FEEL-GOOD SANDWICH AND MY GUILTY PLEASURE, ESPECIALLY AFTER A VERY HECTIC WORK DEADLINE. BRIAN, HOWEVER, THINKS IT'S ABSOLUTELY YUK AND JUST CAN'T UNDERSTAND THE COMBO. I OF COURSE KNOW HE'S WRONG BECAUSE IT'S ABSOLUTELY DELICIOUS!

PREPARATION TIME: 5 MIN
COOKING TIME: 5 MIN
SERVES 1

20ml butter
2ml ground cinnamon
pinch of ground nutmeg
pinch of allspice
pinch of ground cloves
1 or 2 small
bananas, sliced lengthways
2 slices white sourdough bread
30ml crunchy peanut butter

SERVE WITH
scoop of vanilla ice cream

METHOD

In a medium-sized frying pan, heat the butter until melted, add the spices and cook for a minute.

Add the banana halves with the cut-sides down and cook for up to 2 minutes on each side.

Toast the bread and place on a serving plate. Spread the peanut butter on each side. Top with the spiced bananas and ice cream.

Drizzle the spiced butter juices all over the sandwich and enjoy.

SOMETHING SWEET

SCAN TO WATCH
A VIDEO ON
HOW TO
MAKE THIS RECIPE

Siba's tip...
You need to eat this sandwich as soon as it's made, and you'll also need a napkin as the butter juices drip with every bite.

BRAAIED FRUIT KEBABS IN LIME SUGAR

When we braai, we usually serve lots of food. So, a heavy dessert isn't really necessary. In fact, I prefer a light dessert after eating all that meat, sides and salads. These fruit kebabs fit the bill perfectly, especially when served with good chocolate ice cream. They're delicious and each person can braai their own while gathered around the fire, just as you do with marshmallows on sticks.

PREPARATION TIME: 10 MIN
COOKING TIME: 5-7 MIN
SERVES 6

zest of 4 limes
45ml caster sugar
2 pineapples, peeled and cut
into neat pieces
4 peaches, cut into wedges
6 strawberries, halved
6 wooden skewers

SERVE WITH
scoops of good-quality
chocolate ice cream
zest of 2 limes

METHOD

Combine the lime zest and sugar and sprinkle over both sides of all the fruit pieces. Spike all the fruits onto the wooden skewers, alternating with the different fruit pieces. Place on a large flat plate.

Braai for 5 minutes until slightly charred, then turn and braai the other side for 2 more minutes.

Transfer onto serving plates, with scoops of chocolate ice cream on the side. As a final touch, sprinkle with lime zest and serve before the ice cream melts.

Siba's tip...
The wooden skewers need to be soaked in hot water for at least 30 minutes before use, otherwise they'll catch alight and burn on the braai. You can also grill these fruit kebabs on a hot griddle pan brushed with butter, on the stove. And if you want to be a bit fancy, serve them with dark chocolate mousse instead of the ice cream.

PEANUT BUTTER CHOCOLATE BROWNIES

OKAY, CONFESSION! I LOVE PEANUT BUTTER OR PB AS WE CALL IT AT HOME. I WAS WANTING TO REVAMP MY DARK CHOCOLATE BROWNIE RECIPE, SO I PLAYED AROUND IN THE KITCHEN TRYING THIS AND THAT. I EVENTUALLY DECIDED TO LEAVE THE RECIPE AS IT WAS BUT TO LACE THE BROWNIES WITH PEANUT BUTTER SAUCE AND STRAWBERRIES. NOT ONLY DO THEY LOOK GREAT NOW, THEY TASTE EXTRA YUMMY TOO.

PREPARATION TIME: 15 MIN
BAKING TIME: 30-35 MIN
MAKES 12

250g 60% dark chocolate
125ml butter
125ml sugar
125ml dark brown sugar
3 extra-large eggs
5ml vanilla extract
180ml all-purpose flour
pinch of salt

TOPPING
80ml crunchy peanut butter
30ml hot milk
2ml vanilla pod, scraped out (optional)
50ml white chocolate shavings, melted

GARNISH
6 strawberries, sliced
white chocolate shavings

METHOD

Melt the chocolate and pour it into a large bowl. Stir in the butter and both sugars, adding them a little at a time, and beating until well mixed.

Add the eggs, one at a time, and beat the mixture after each addition. Stir in the vanilla extract.

Season the flour with the salt and gently fold it into the chocolate mixture. Scrape onto a lightly greased 20x30cm baking tin and place on a rack that's one lower than the centre. (A 25cm square baking tin will yield slightly thicker brownies.)

Bake for 30-35 minutes until the brownie mixture starts moving away from the sides of the pan or a few crumbs come out when tested with a cocktail stick.

Using a palate knife, place on a cooling rack to cool down completely. Once cooled, cut into 12 slices.

To make the topping, place all the ingredients in a saucepan and heat until combined, adding more milk if the mixture is too thick. Once cool, roughly spread teaspoonfuls of the mixture on each brownie. Garnish with strawberry slices and white chocolate shavings.

Siba's tip...
Brownies should be soft and gooey in the centre and not cake like, so take care not to overbake them. Though the scraped vanilla pod is optional, it really does add something special, and if you don't have a vanilla pod then you can use 5ml of vanilla extract.

'CHEAT' TRUFFLES

THESE CHOCOLATE COATED BISCUIT BALLS ARE A REAL CHEAT! THEY LOOK AND TASTE AMAZING AND ARE EASY TO MAKE TOO. I HAVE CHOPPED AND CHANGED THIS RECIPE SO MANY TIMES BUT HAVE DECIDED TO STICK TO MY ORIGINAL VERSION TO MAKE THIS KID FRIENDLY.

PREPARATION TIME: 20 MIN
COOKING TIME: 5 MIN
MAKES 16+

250g (1 packet) tea biscuits
125ml desiccated coconut, toasted
30ml butter, melted
340g can sweetened condensed milk

COAT IN
dark and/white chocolate, melted
desiccated coconut

METHOD

In a food processor, crush the biscuits until very fine. Place in a bowl and mix with the toasted coconut.

Add the melted butter and condensed milk, a little at a time, until the consistency is suitable enough to roll balls in your hands, using a heaped teaspoonful at a time. Place on greaseproof paper.

Tip the melted chocolate into a bowl and gently roll the truffles until evenly coated. Then roll them in either dark or lightly toasted coconut. Place on a plate lined with greaseproof paper and cover with plastic wrap. Chill until set or set aside in a cool place to dry.

Siba's tip...
These make a great gift for someone special and can be stored in a jar once they've set. They're also very easy to make – you just need a bit of time, and maybe help, to roll them into balls and dip them in the chocolate. Children will have fun helping you make these delightful cheat chocolate truffle bites.

SOMETHING SWEET

WHO DOESN'T LOVE SOMETHING **SWEET?** A LITTLE TREAT AFTER DINNER... AN AFTER LUNCH PICK-ME-UP?

YUM!!

LABNEH

This is a soft cheese made from yoghurt. I know, when most people hear homemade cheese they think lots of work, but I kid you not, this is unbelievably easy to make. All you have to do is strain good-quality thick yoghurt for a day or so, and there it is — your own cheese. That's all there is to it! I've experimented many times with this recipe, using flavoured yoghurts and even infusing flavour into plain yoghurts for a slightly different result. It's something I picked up during my travels in the Middle East and just fell in love with.

PREPARATION TIME: 25 MIN
NO COOKING TIME
WAITING TIME: 12-24 HRS
SERVES 4

2 litres double-thick
Greek yoghurt
60ml honey, plus extra
to drizzle
1 vanilla pod, seeds scraped out
or 5ml vanilla extract

SAUCE
125g raspberries
30ml icing sugar

SERVE WITH
100g strawberries, sliced
150g cherries, halved
50g blueberries
30ml honey, to drizzle
30g pistachio nuts, chopped
(optional)

METHOD

Combine the yogurt, honey and vanilla. Place two colanders on top of two separate mixing bowls and line each colander with muslin cloth or a thin tea towel.

Divide the yoghurt mixture in two and spoon onto the cloth in the colanders. Bring the sides of the cloth together and tie a tight knot at the top. Insert a wooden spoon under the knot and then rest the spoon on the colander so that the balls are suspended above the bottom.

The liquid from the yoghurt will start dripping through the cloth and colander into the dish below. Leave both balls like this overnight or for a day. Once thoroughly drained, discard the whey that has collected in the bowls below, and remove the yoghurt from the cloth. Place on two individual plates.

In a blender, whizz the raspberries and icing sugar to make the sauce. Drizzle the raspberry sauce over the labneh and scatter the berries. Drizzle over the honey, and sprinkle with nuts to garnish and serve.

SCAN TO WATCH
A VIDEO ON
HOW TO
MAKE THIS RECIPE

Siba's tip...

I use double-thick Greek yoghurt, which results in quite a firm, creamy cheese consistency. You can also use plain or low-fat yoghurt, which will make a softer, less creamy cheese. You can drain the labneh for fewer hours and use it as a dip infused with roasted garlic and fresh herbs such as thyme and marjoram, and lemon zest. The QR code gives another version of this dish that's worth checking out.

FRIED ICE CREAM

I CALL THIS A NAUGHTY TREAT, AND WHEN I TALK ABOUT IT PEOPLE ALWAYS FURROW THEIR BROWS BECAUSE THE IDEA OF FRYING ICE CREAM SEEMS ABSURD. I FIRST HAD FRIED ICE CREAM IN A FANCY RESTAURANT YEARS AGO WHEN I WAS STILL A STUDENT. IT WAS SERVED IN A LIGHT SWEET AND SPICY BATTER. THE IDEA OF SUCH A DESSERT INTRIGUED ME AND I HAVE SINCE EXPERIMENTED A LOT WITH IT. I USE COCONUT OIL FOR FRYING AS IT PROVIDES A MUCH MORE DELICIOUS FLAVOUR THAN ANY OTHER OIL. OF COURSE IT'S BEST TO SERVE THIS DESSERT AS SOON AS IT COMES OUT OF THE PAN.

PREPARATION TIME: 10 MIN
COOKING TIME: 5 MIN
FREEZING TIME: 2 HRS +
SERVES 6

1 litre vanilla ice cream
50g walnuts, chopped
50g hazelnuts, chopped
60ml salty and crunchy
pretzels, crushed
60ml dried cranberries, chopped
coconut oil, for frying

COATING
125g corn flakes
100g tea biscuits
75ml desiccated
coconut, toasted
1 egg white, lightly whisked

GARNISH
30g pistachio nuts, chopped

METHOD

Line a baking tray with plastic wrap. Mix the ice cream with the chopped nuts, pretzels and dried cranberries. Then scoop it into balls using an ice cream scoop and gently place them on the lined baking tray. Freeze until rock solid for 2 hours or so.

In a food processor, blend the corn flakes and biscuits together and tip into a bowl. Mix with the toasted coconut and place on a flat plate. Place the egg white in a shallow soup plate too.

Remove the ice cream from the freezer and, working fast, coat the balls in the dry mix, egg white and dry mix again, shaping them into evenly rounded balls. Return them onto the tray and back to the freezer for an hour or two, until they're rock solid again.

Heat the coconut oil until it's hot enough to fry, and fry one or two ice cream balls at a time for 10–20 seconds, turning once or twice. Remove from the heat and serve immediately in bowls or martini glasses. Continue frying and serving, until you finish. Garnish with the chopped nuts.

Siba's tip...
Don't worry if the ice cream balls go flat at the bottom after first being frozen because they'll be molded into balls when you coat them. I sometimes serve this with melted hazelnut spread.

STRAWBERRY, ALMOND + COCONUT BAKE

I MAKE THIS FOR PICNICS AND ALFRESCO LUNCHES AND IT'S A POPULAR FAVOURITE AT HOME, AMONG MY FRIENDS AND EXTENDED FAMILY. WHENEVER I'M GATHERING WITH FRIENDS AND TASKED WITH BRINGING AN EASY DESSERT, I OPT FOR THIS BAKE AS IT'S EASY TO CARRY AND ALWAYS A HIT!

PREPARATION TIME: 20 MIN
COOKING TIME: 35 MIN
MAKES 12 SLICES

325ml butter, room temperature
750ml all-purpose flour
7ml baking powder
pinch of salt
200ml caster sugar
240ml desiccated coconut
cold water to bind

FILLING
300g strawberry jam
350g strawberries, sliced

TOPPING
2 extra-large eggs
100ml sugar
180ml rolled oats
75g flaked almonds
60ml desiccated coconut

METHOD

Preheat the oven to 180°C and lightly grease a 20x30cm baking tin. Place the butter in a large bowl. Mix the flour with the baking powder and salt and add it to the butter. Rub together until the mixture resembles breadcrumbs.

Add the sugar and desiccated coconut and mix to combine, adding a splash of cold water to turn the mixture into a dough. Remove from the bowl and press into the base of the baking tin. Prick with a fork and bake for 15–20 minutes until golden, then leave to cool.

Spread the jam over the cooled base and top with the sliced strawberries. Beat the eggs until frothy, using an electric beater, then add the sugar and beat until light and fluffy for about 5 minutes.

Gently add the oats, flaked almonds and coconut into the egg and sugar mix until combined. Pour over the base and jam filling. Bake for a further 15 minutes or until the top is golden. Set aside to cool in the tin. Cut into squares and serve.

SCAN TO WATCH
A VIDEO ON
HOW TO
MAKE THIS RECIPE

Siba's tip...
You can leave the coconut out of the shortbread base and replace it with the juice and zest of a lime for a citrus flavour, or pecan nuts and cinnamon for a nutty taste.

LEMON POSSET

I OFTEN HAVE THIS DESSERT AT ONE OF MY FAVOURITE RESTAURANTS IN CAPE TOWN, CHEF'S WAREHOUSE ON BREE STREET. IT'S SO LOVELY THAT I DECIDED TO GO HOME AND TRY IT MYSELF, ESPECIALLY SINCE THE CHEF LIAM TOMLIN WAS GENEROUS ENOUGH TO SHARE HIS RECIPE WITH ME. IT REQUIRES ONLY A HANDFUL OF SIMPLE INGREDIENTS AND YOU CAN REALLY GO WILD SUBSTITUTING THE FRUIT TOPPING WITH OTHER FLAVOURS, SUCH AS PEACH AND PASSION FRUIT OR VANILLA POD POACHED PEARS. MINE IS TOPPED WITH A RASPBERRY COULIS, A TASTE I FIND HARD TO RESIST.

 ## METHOD

PREPARATION TIME: 5 MIN
COOKING TIME: 10 MIN
SERVES 8

1 litre double cream
300ml caster sugar
juice of 4 lemons
5ml vanilla extract

RASPBERRY COULIS
500g raspberries
75ml icing sugar

GARNISH
250g raspberries
125g blueberries
icing sugar, to dust

In a medium-sized saucepan, heat the cream and sugar, stirring continuously until the sugar has dissolved. Bring to the boil and simmer for 5 minutes over medium heat. Remove from the heat, whisk in the lemon juice and stir in the vanilla last.

Place the mixture aside for 5 minutes and then skim any froth that has formed on top. Strain and pour into short glasses, placed on a tray to steady them, and leave to cool down completely. Cover with plastic wrap and chill in the fridge overnight, or for a day, until set.

To make the coulis, whizz the raspberries and icing sugar in a blender. Pour spoonfuls of the mixture into each glass and garnish with the raspberries and blueberries. Dust with icing sugar and serve.

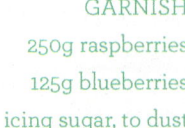
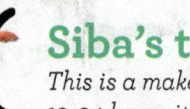

Siba's tip...
This is a make-ahead dessert, so be sure to allow for the 12–24 hours it needs to set. Since it's quite rich, it's best served in small quantities, so use short glasses but leave enough space for the fruit topping.

every mouthful is
a taste of heaven!

RED VELVET CAKE

I LOVE LAVISH DESSERTS AND AS FAR AS I'M CONCERNED, RED VELVET CAKE IS THE EPITOME OF LAVISH. I ONLY BAKE IT ON SPECIAL OCCASIONS AS IT NEEDS QUITE A BIT OF TIME AND ATTENTION TO MAKE. THIS RECIPE MAKES FOUR GENEROUS LAYERS AND I LOVE THE TOUCH OF SOURNESS IN THE FROSTING THAT BALANCES THE SWEETNESS OF THE CAKE.

PREPARATION TIME: 40 MIN
BAKING TIME: 30-40 MIN
COOLING TIME: 20-30 MIN
MAKES A 4-LAYER CAKE

4 x 250ml all-purpose flour
20ml baking powder
40ml cocoa powder
5ml salt
165ml butter, room temperature
660ml caster sugar
350ml canola oil
6 extra-large eggs, separated
20ml vanilla extract
7ml white wine vinegar
20ml red food colouring
325ml buttermilk, room temperature

CREAM CHEESE ICING
2 x 250g tubs plain cream cheese
160ml butter, room temperature
1,25 litres icing sugar
juice of 1 lemon
10ml vanilla extract
mixed berries, to garnish

METHOD

Preheat the oven to 175°C. Lightly grease two 20cm loose-bottomed cake tins. Mix the flour, baking powder, cocoa and salt together in a large mixing bowl. Using an electric beater, cream the butter and sugar until light and creamy.

Keep the beater on and gradually add the oil until well combined. Don't worry if the mixture looks like it's going to split, that's normal. Add the egg yolks and vanilla and keep beating until well combined.

Scrape down the sides with a spatula and add the vinegar. Then add the food colouring, just a few drops at a time, until you've achieved a bright red colour or one that you're happy with. Turn the beater to slow and sift in the dry ingredients in three batches, alternating with buttermilk, but starting and ending with the dry ingredients. Take care not to overmix.

In a separate bowl mix the egg whites with the beater, until soft peaks appear. Carefully fold the egg whites into the cake batter. Divide the batter between the 2 baking tins and bake for 30–45 minutes or until a skewer comes out clean.

If still very moist, bake for a further 5–7 minutes, but take care not to overbake as this should be a moist cake. Remove from the oven and allow the cakes to cool on a cooling rack. Once the cakes have cooled, slice each cake into two layers, so that you have 4 layers in total.

To make the cream cheese icing: In a large bowl, whisk the cream cheese and butter together until smooth. Add the icing sugar, lemon juice and vanilla extract, whisking all the time until smooth. Use a palette knife to spread the icing onto each layer and then decorate the top and sides of the cake with the icing. Garnish with berries.

Siba's tip...
The cake needs to cool down completely before being iced, otherwise the icing will melt. If you prefer a sweeter icing, the lemon juice can be substituted with the same amount of milk.

MY RED VELVET DELIGHT

THIS IS A CHEAT CAKE THAT I MAKE WITH STORE-BOUGHT RED VELVET CAKE WHEN I DON'T HAVE TIME TO BAKE MY OWN. ONCE I PUT MY SPIN ON IT, THOUGH, HARDLY ANYONE NOTICES THAT IT'S STORE-BOUGHT. IT SUDDENLY BECOMES A CAKE WITH A LOT OF PIZZAZZ.

PREPARATION TIME: 15-20 MIN
NO COOKING TIME
SERVES 8

1 red velvet cake with sour cream frosting, three layers

FILLING
400ml cream
45ml caster sugar
5ml vanilla extract
juice of 1 or 2 lemons
500g raspberries
500g strawberries, sliced
a few blueberries, sliced
a few gooseberries, sliced

GARNISH
white vanilla extract chocolate shavings
pomegranate rubies
icing sugar, to dust

METHOD

Carefully slice each layer of the cake horizontally, creating 6 layers instead of 3. Don't separate the layers that were joined by icing when you bought the cake.

Whip the cream with the sugar, vanilla extract and lemon juice. In a large bowl mix the raspberries and sliced strawberries together.

To assemble the delight, place one of the layers without icing on a cake stand. Spread over a layer of whipped cream and top with a quarter of the mixed berries.

Now place a layer containing the store-bought icing on top of the cream and berries. Once again spread over the cream and add the berries.

Place the second layer of cake with the store-bought icing on top of the cream and berries. Spread a further layer of cream and berries. Then place the final plain layer of cake on top of that and repeat the cream and berry topping.

Loosely sprinkle the white chocolate shavings and the pomegranate rubies over the berries and cream. Dust with icing sugar just before serving.

SCAN TO WATCH
A VIDEO ON
HOW TO
MAKE THIS RECIPE

Siba's tip...
You can use a two-layer cake as well for this recipe. Be careful when cutting through the layers not to break them or puncture the cake. Cream cheese is steadier than cream, so if you're not going to serve the cake immediately, use cream cheese instead of cream.

just keep going, layer after layer.

ICE CREAM CAKE

I found ice cream irresistible for a long time, but I've since decided to go for homemade sorbets. When I was still in the thrall of ice cream, I used to mix my favourite ingredients into ice cream. And then, at some point, I came up with the idea of making an ice cream cake with ganache poured over it. The nut and cherry garnishes came as an experimental afterthought. It worked extremely well and looked lovely too. It's something different, something unexpected and a must-have in summer!

PREPARATION TIME: 15 MIN
FREEZING TIME: 4-8 HRS
COOKING TIME: 5 MIN
SERVES 6

2-litres soft-serve vanilla ice cream
60g pecans, roughly chopped
60g flaked almonds, toasted
60g macadamia nuts,
roughly chopped
125ml maraschino cherries, drained
and chopped

TOPPING
100g 60% cocoa dark chocolate
125ml cream
15ml pistachio nuts, chopped
15ml flaked almonds, toasted
6 maraschino cherries with stalks,
to garnish

METHOD

In a large bowl, mix the ice cream with the nuts and cherries. Transfer into a 20cm silicon cake mould, and smooth the top. Transfer to the freezer for 4 hours or overnight until rock solid.

For the ganache topping, break the chocolate into pieces and place in a heatproof bowl over a pan of simmering water, to melt. Once melted, remove from the heat and stir in the cream. Leave to cool slightly.

To serve, remove the frozen ice cream cake from the freezer. Invert on a serving platter and carefully peel off the silicon mould. Smooth any imperfections with a spatula or palette knife.

Pour the chocolate ganache onto the centre of the cake. Sprinkle the nuts over the top. Top with the cherries, and cut into slices and serve immediately.

Siba's tip...
The ice cream cake must be rock hard when the ganache is poured over it, and the ganache must've cooled slightly beforehand.

POPCORN ICE CREAM CAKE

THIS RECIPE CAME ABOUT LAST SUMMER WHILE I WAS CHILLING WITH MY BOYS IN THE GARDEN. WE WERE HAVING PEANUT BUTTER AND JAM ICE CREAM, AND LONWABO HAD THE ADDITIONAL TREAT OF A BOWL OF POPCORN. BRIAN PLAYFULLY ADDED SOME POPCORN TO HIS ICE CREAM AND WAS PLEASANTLY SURPRISED. WHEN HE OFFERED ME A TASTE, THE IDEA FOR THIS CAKE IMMEDIATELY POPPED INTO MY MIND. I DECIDED TO STEER CLEAR OF THE PEANUT BUTTER AND JAM, GOING FOR A SALTED CARAMEL POPCORN BASE SMEARED WITH CHOCOLATE INSTEAD. THE LEMON CURD BALANCES THE SWEETNESS OF THE ICE CREAM AND CARAMEL POPCORN.

PREPARATION TIME: 15 MIN
COOKING TIME: 15 MIN
CHILLING TIME: 10 MIN
SERVES UP TO 12

CARAMEL SYRUP
125ml butter
250ml sugar
60ml honey
375ml milk
pinch of salt

POPCORN CHOCOLATE SPREAD
100g salted popcorn, popped
100g pecan nuts, toasted and roughly chopped
200g 60% dark chocolate, broken into pieces and melted
15ml butter

MIX WITH
2 litres good-quality vanilla ice cream, softened but not melted

SERVE WITH
250ml store-bought lemon curd

METHOD

Place the butter, sugar, honey, milk and salt in a large saucepan. Over a low heat, stir until the sugar has dissolved and then bring to the boil. Simmer over medium heat for 10 minutes, until the syrup is a deep golden brown and has thickened. Set aside.

Tip the popcorn and nuts into the caramel syrup and mix until they are coated. Divide into three and reserve one third. Press each of the remaining thirds onto greased 20cm loose-bottom cake tins to form two popcorn disks. Mix the melted chocolate with the butter and divide between the two, smearing all over to cover each base. Leave to cool.

Scoop half the ice cream onto one popcorn disk, levelling with a spoon. Top with the second popcorn disk and then scoop the remaining ice cream onto that, levelling with a spoon. Freeze overnight, until rock hard. To assemble, place the cake on a cake stand or a beautiful plate. Drizzle generously with lemon curd and garnish with the reserved third of caramel popcorn. Serve immediately.

Siba's tip...
Adding butter to the chocolate softens it so it's easy to cut, otherwise it becomes rock solid when frozen. It's important that the chocolate covers the popcorn base, as it protects the popcorn from becoming soft and soggy from the ice cream. The salted caramel popcorn can be eaten as a snack on its own.

LOCAL IS *LE

KKER

My celebration of some of South Africa's popular dishes...

& some with a twist

South African colloquial word derived from Afrikaans that means delicious, awesome or nice!

erewors

THE NAME BOEREWORS IS DERIVED FROM THE AFRIKAANS WORDS BOER (FARMER) AND WORS (SAUSAGE) AND WAS INTRODUCED TO SOUTH AFRICA BY THE EARLY DUTCH SETTLERS, WHO, LIKE MOST EUROPEANS, WERE SAUSAGE MAKERS OF NOTE. BOEREWORS MUST CONTAIN AT LEAST 90% MEAT — MAINLY BEEF WITH A SMALLER AMOUNT OF PORK OR LAMB. ONE CAN ALSO ADD A MIXTURE OF PORK AND LAMB TO THE BEEF. IT IS SPICED MAINLY WITH CRUSHED WHOLE CORIANDER SEEDS, GROUND CLOVES, ALLSPICE, NUTMEG, SALT AND PEPPER ALONG WITH VINEGAR AND SOMETIMES CEREAL OR STARCH FOR BINDING. THE SAUSAGE MEAT IS STUFFED INTO EITHER A PORK OR LAMB CASING.

BOEREWORS IS A MUST FOR EVERY BRAAI. AND BY BRAAI I MEAN FOOD COOKED ON COALS, NOT A GAS GRILL OR GAS BARBEQUE! WHEN BRAAING OR COOKING, IT'S BEST NOT TO POKE OR PUNCTURE THE BOEREWORS WITH A FORK AS ITS FAT WILL OOZE OUT BEFORE IT COOKS AND CAUSE IT TO BECOME DRY. IT'S ALSO BETTER TO SLIGHTLY UNDERCOOK IT AND ALLOW THE HEAT FROM INSIDE THE SAUSAGE TO CONTINUE COOKING IT, TO PREVENT OVERCOOKING AND DRYING OUT. BY THE WAY, BY UNDERCOOKING I DON'T MEAN THE SAUSAGE SHOULD BE RAW IN THE CENTRE, RATHER JUST VERY SLIGHTY PINK. THIS SAUSAGE MAKES A GREAT COMPANION FOR OTHER MEAT COOKED ON THE BRAAI AND A MEAN BRAAIED BOERIE-ROLL WITH SAUTÉED ONION AND SAUCE. I ALSO REMOVE ITS CASING AND USE THE MEAT TO MAKE BURGER PATTIES AND THE MOST DELICIOUS BOBOTIE EVER (SEE RECIPE ON THE NEXT PAGE)!

BOEREWORS BOBOTIE

WHEN I DO FOOD DEMONSTRATIONS OVERSEAS, I OFTEN FIND THAT BOBOTIE IS ONE OF THE VERY FEW DISHES PEOPLE RECOGNISE AS BEING FROM SOUTH AFRICA. SINCE THIS SECTION IS ALL ABOUT CELEBRATING LOCAL FOOD, I THOUGHT I'D GIVE IT A TWIST BY ADDING ANOTHER FAMOUS SOUTH AFRICAN INGREDIENT — BOEREWORS. PEOPLE WHO ARE NOT FAMILIAR WITH OUR LOCAL CUISINE ARE USUALLY INTRIGUED BY THIS UNUSUAL SAUSAGE, WANTING TO KNOW HOW TO PRONOUNCE THE NAME AND WHAT IT'S MADE OF. USING IT TO MAKE BOBOTIE IS REALLY LOVELY AS LONG AS YOU DON'T OVER-SEASON THE DISH BECAUSE THE SAUSAGE IS ALREADY SEASONED.

PREPARATION TIME: 15 MIN
COOKING TIME: 1.5 HRS
SERVES 8

3 slices brown bread, crust removed
500ml full cream milk, warmed
30ml olive oil
10ml butter
1 large onion, finely chopped
3 cloves garlic, crushed
15ml mild curry powder
7ml turmeric
30ml apricot chutney
15ml apricot jam
15ml Worcestershire sauce
30ml apple cider vinegar
750g boerewors, casing removed
250g lean beef mince
5ml salt and freshly ground black pepper, to taste
80ml raisins
3 eggs
a few dried bay leaves
flaked almonds, toasted, to garnish

METHOD

Place the bread on a shallow plate and pour the milk over it to soak for about 10 minutes. Heat the butter and oil in a large frying pan and sauté the onions and garlic for 4 minutes, until soft and translucent but not yet browned.

Add the curry powder and half the turmeric and cook for a minute. Add the chutney, jam, Worcestershire sauce and vinegar, and stir well to combine. In a bowl, mix the boerewors (casing removed) with the mince and then add it to the spiced onion mixture in three batches, flaking it with a fork. Keep the heat high and make sure each batch is browned before adding the next one.

Drain the bread and add it to the mixture along with the raisins, reserving the milk for later. Transfer to an oven dish. In a jug, beat the eggs with the reserved milk, the rest of the turmeric and lightly season. Pour over the mince mixture and place a few bay leaves on top.

Place the dish in a bain-marie (a roasting pan half-filled with hot water), making sure the water won't spill into the dish. Gently place in the oven to bake for 45 min to 1 hour or until the egg mixture is set. Remove from the oven and top with the toasted almonds. Serve while still warm with rice, veggies of your choice, tomato salsa and chutney.

Siba's tip...
I find it really helps to have the bain-marie as the water cools the dry oven air down, thereby preventing the cooked mince from drying out and overcooking. You can replace the raisins with sultanas or cranberries, or a mixture of both, for a slightly different flavour.

BRAAIED SNOEK

Whenever we travelled back to the Eastern Cape from Cape Town during our holidays, we'd always pack snoek for padkos or umphako (translated as food for the road). This bony but fleshy fish is synonymous with the Western Cape and whenever we have visitors who are unfamiliar with the Cape, I make sure that braaied snoek is served. This recipe sees it braaied in the customary way, with a spicy apricot jam glaze. This is as local as local gets.

METHOD

PREPARATION TIME: 10 MIN
COOKING TIME: 25 MIN
SERVES 6

1,2kg snoek, cleaned with head and tail removed
sea salt and freshly ground black pepper

SPICY APRICOT GLAZE
80g butter
4 large cloves garlic, crushed
1 small red chili, deseeded and finely sliced
125ml apricot jam
30ml apricot chutney (optional)
60ml chicken or fish stock
45ml fresh coriander, chopped
juice of 1 lemon

Prepare a fire for the braai and wait until the coals are gentle enough to cook over. Pat the snoek dry and place it skin-side down on a sheet of tin foil. Liberally season with salt and pepper.

In a saucepan, heat the butter and sauté the garlic for a minute until fragrant. Add the chili and stir. Add the jam, chutney and stock, stirring vigorously to combine, then reduce the heat and simmer for 5 minutes.

Stir in the coriander and cook for a minute. Remove from the heat and transfer to a jug. Place the snoek (still on the foil) on the braai and, using a basting brush, generously smear the fish with the glaze. Cook for 8-10 minutes on the skin side.

When the fish turns white, turn and baste it, and cook it for 3–5 minutes on the other side. For a smoky flavour, you could braai the other side without the foil, making sure the grid is well oiled to prevent the fish from sticking to it. If you do this, reduce the cooking time to 2–3 minutes and watch the fish closely.

Siba's tip...
When buying fresh snoek, ask to have it cleaned. Then, before braaing it, it's important to wash and pat it dry well with a paper towel or clean cloth. You can bake snoek in the oven instead of braaing it, but make sure the oven is set to grill and move the fish to one of the higher racks to allow it to brown nicely. Snoek has lots of bones but the great thing is that most are long and easily identifiable.

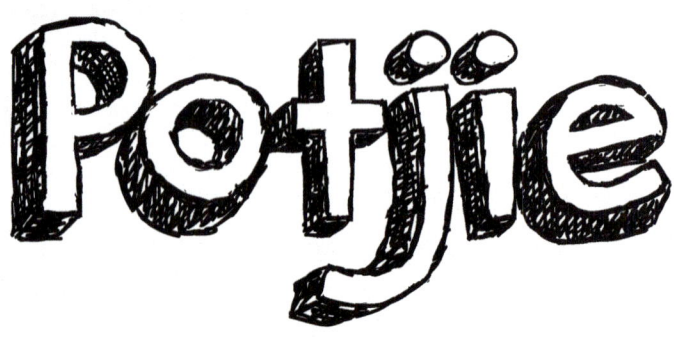

Potjie

THE WELL-KNOWN AND POPULAR THREE-LEGGED CAST-IRON
POT WE CALL A 'POTJIE' IN AFRIKAANS AND A 'NOPOTYI'
IN XHOSA DOES NOT ORIGINATE IN SOUTHERN OR SOUTH
AFRICA. IT WAS ACTUALLY INTRODUCED TO US BY THE
DUTCH BUT HAS SINCE BECOME DEEPLY EMBEDDED IN OUR
TRADITIONAL FOOD CULTURE. DIRECTLY TRANSLATED IT
MEANS 'SMALL POT' AND 'POTJIEKOS' MEANS 'FOOD MADE
IN A SMALL POT'. (THE STRANGE THING IS, THOUGH, THAT
A POTJIE IS NOT REALLY ALL THAT SMALL.) SIMPLY PUT,
POTJIEKOS IS STEW COOKED IN THIS POT BUT IT REALLY IS
A STEW UNLIKE ANY OTHER AS IT'S THE ACTUAL POT THAT
GIVES IT ITS MAGICAL TASTE AND FLAVOUR!

IF YOU HAVE ONE, IT'S VERY IMPORTANT TO KNOW HOW
TO CLEAN AND STORE IT AS IT WILL HAVE A LONG LIFE IF
YOU TAKE GOOD CARE OF IT. SO MAKE SURE YOU RINSE IT
WITH WARM SOAPY WATER AND DRY IT WELL AFTER USE
TO PREVENT RUSTING. ONCE DRIED, RUB IT WITH A THIN
LAYER OF OIL TO SERVE AS PROTECTION, FILL IT WITH OLD
NEWSPAPER AND PLACE IT IN STORAGE UNTIL ITS NEXT USE.

LAMB NECK POTJIE

My grandparents had a small livestock farm and large gardens, where they grew their own veggies. For them cooking outside on a wood fire was the norm. A potjie (heavy three-legged cast-iron pot) would be used for cooking food, making traditional bread — idombolo or steamed bread as we call it — and sometimes just for boiling large quantities of water. It fascinated me that it was the women who gathered the wood, carried it on their heads in a bundle and lit the fire.

METHOD

In a large bowl, combine the flour, spices, garlic and rosemary seasoning. Roll the lamb neck in the flour and spices to coat, then set aside.

In a medium-sized pojtie over hot coals, heat the canola oil, add the lamb and brown it for 4 minutes. Add the onion, celery, half the garlic and green pepper and sauté for 5 minutes.

Add the remaining seasoned flour from coating the meat and cook for a minute to make a roux-like mixture. Stir in the tomato paste and canned tomatoes. Pour in the stock and season with salt and pepper. Stir again to integrate the ingredients.

Simmer for 1 hour 20 minutes, stirring every 20–30 minutes, adding water if needed, until the meat is tender. Throughout the cooking time check that the coals aren't too hot. If they are, separate them to reduce the heat.

Add the potatoes and carrots and cook for a further 15 minutes until the veggies are cooked but still firm. Add the tomatoes, pickling onions and remaining garlic and cook until done. Serve with crusty bread.

PREPARATION TIME: 15 MIN
COOKING TIME: 2 HRS
SERVES 4

60ml plain flour
10ml ground cumin
10ml smoked paprika
10ml ground coriander
10ml garlic and rosemary dry
seasoning mix
600g lamb neck chops
30ml canola oil
2 onions, halved and sliced
2 celery sticks, sliced
4 cloves garlic, chopped
1 large green pepper, cored
and diced
15ml tomato paste
400g canned tomatoes, chopped
800ml chicken stock
salt and pepper
6 baby potatoes, halved
8 whole baby carrots, washed
6-8 small tomatoes on the vine
5 small pickling onions

SERVE + GARNISH
crusty bread, to serve
fresh parsley, to garnish

Siba's tip...

Traditionally, potjiekos (potjie food) is cooked in a three-legged, cast-iron pot over coals outdoors and it's this way of cooking that gives the dish its particular flavour. If you don't have a potjie, you can use a flat Dutch pot, either on the coals or the stove. If you don't have either of these, then use a heavy-based pot on the stove to make a lamb neck stew rather than a lamb neck potjie.

CHAKALAKA

THIS IS A WONDERFUL AND VERY PROUDLY SOUTH AFRICAN RELISH. IT'S A WELL-KNOWN COMPANION FOR MEAT AND SALADS AT A BRAAI. THE CURRY POWDER AND CHILI MAKE IT A BIT SPICY, BUT THOSE CAN BE CONTROLLED BY USING A MILDER CURRY AND REMOVING THE PITH AND SEEDS OF THE CHILI. THE GRATED GINGER IS A DELIGHTFUL SURPRISE, AND GIVES THIS RELISH A FRESH KICK. I LIKE ADDING A CAN OF BAKED BEANS AT THE END, BUT DOING THAT IS OPTIONAL.

PREPARATION TIME: 20 MIN
COOKING TIME: 20 MIN
SERVES 6+

15ml olive oil
1 onion, finely chopped
2 cloves garlic, crushed
2 bird's eye chilies, deseeded
and chopped
50ml ginger, finely grated
30ml mild curry powder
1 green pepper, finely chopped
1 red pepper, finely chopped
1 yellow pepper, finely chopped
5 large carrots, scrubbed, topped
and tailed and grated
3ml tomato purée
400g can chopped and
peeled tomatoes
400g can baked beans (optional)
2 sprigs fresh thyme, leaves only
sea salt and freshly ground black
pepper, to taste

METHOD

In a large frying pan, heat the oil and fry the onion for 2 minutes until soft and translucent. Add the garlic, chilies and half of the ginger – reserve the other half to add right at the end. Add the curry powder and stir to combine.

Add the peppers and fry for another 2 minutes, followed by the carrots. Stir well to make sure they are coated in the curry powder.

Add the tomato purée and tomatoes and stir. Cook for 5-10 minutes until the mixture is well combined and slightly thickened.

Remove from the heat, add the baked beans, fresh thyme, remaining ginger and seasoning to taste, and stir to combine. Serve warm or cold.

Siba's tip...

Chakalaka keeps well in the fridge and can last for up to a week, and longer, if kept in a sealed container. If you plan to freeze it, be sure to reduce the cooking time and undercook the veggies to allow for reheating when it has thawed. Since the beans are added at the end of the cooking process, freezing them won't cause them to split once reheated. And, since ginger loses its flavour when cooked for a long time, it's important to reserve half the ginger to add at the end and ensure its flavour won't be lost.

SCAN TO WATCH
A VIDEO ON
HOW TO
MAKE THIS RECIPE

SEAFOOD BUNNY CHOW

A 'BUNNY CHOW' OR 'QUARTER', AS THIS DELICIOUS CURRY IN HOLLOWED-OUT BREAD IS KNOWN, HAS ITS ROOTS IN THE INDIAN CULTURE OF KWAZULU-NATAL. IN THE EASTERN CAPE IT'S POPULARLY KNOWN AS A 'IKOTA' (REFERRING TO A QUARTER OF A LOAF) THAT IS USUALLY FILLED WITH BEAN, BEEF, MUTTON OR CHICKEN CURRY. MINE IS A FANCIER VERSION, USING PRAWNS, MUSSELS AND CALAMARI IN A WONDERFULLY RICH AND FRAGRANT CURRY SAUCE. THE BREAD IS REPLACED WITH WHOLEWHEAT GOURMET ROLLS.

PREPARATION TIME: 20 MIN
COOKING TIME: 25 MIN
SERVES 6

45ml olive oil
1 red onion, finely chopped
2 cloves garlic, crushed
5ml fresh ginger, grated
1 red chili, seeded and chopped
5ml garam masala
5ml crushed coriander seeds
2ml each of turmeric, paprika
and ground cumin
15ml tomato paste
400g can chopped, peeled tomatoes
400g can coconut milk
250ml chicken stock
salt, black pepper and sugar

SEAFOOD MIXTURE
2 cloves garlic, crushed
5ml fresh ginger, grated
30ml korma paste
400g calamari tubes, cut into rings
250g prawns, shelled
250g mussels, rinsed and shelled
5ml soy sauce, to season

SERVE WITH
4-6 wholewheat gourmet rolls
¼ red onion, very thinly sliced
fresh coriander leaves, rinsed

METHOD

Scoop out the insides of the rolls to make hollows for filling and cover until needed. Heat 30ml of the olive oil in a large saucepan with a lid and sauté the onion and garlic for 2 minutes until soft and translucent. Add the ginger and chili and stir.

Add the spices and heat for a minute to release their flavour. Stir in the tomato paste and season well with salt and pepper.

Pour in the canned tomatoes, coconut milk and chicken stock, and bring to the boil. Half cover and simmer gently for 15-20 minutes, until the sauce is fragrant and has thickened slightly. Season lightly with salt, pepper and sugar for taste.

In the meantime, heat the rest of the oil in a large frying pan and sauté the garlic and ginger for a minute. Stir in the korma paste. Add the seafood mixture, season with the soy sauce and sauté for 2 minutes, until almost cooked.

Transfer this mixture to the simmering curry sauce pot, stirring until combined, and cook for a further 2 minutes until the seafood is cooked. Spoon the curry mixture into the hollowed-out rolls and garnish with red onion slices and coriander. Serve with chutney or tomato salsa.

Siba's tip...
When simmering the curry sauce, make sure it doesn't thicken too much by adding some water or more chicken or fish stock when necessary. It's best to add the seafood mix to the curry sauce before it's fully cooked so it can absorb the curry flavour. Remember that seafood cooks in less than 5 minutes and shouldn't be overcooked, otherwise it'll become tough and rubbery, especially calamari.

SEVEN-COLOUR RICE

IT'S BECOME A KIND OF TRADITION THAT MY SUNDAY MEALS ARE COLOURFUL AND VIBRANT. THIS SAVOURY RICE GOES WELL WITH MOST TYPES OF MEAT AND A RANGE OF SIDE VEGETABLES, SALADS AND GRAVIES, SO IT REALLY IS A VERSATILE ACCOMPANIMENT FOR THAT TRADITIONAL SUNDAY MEAL.

PREPARATION TIME: 10 MIN
COOKING TIME: 20 MIN
SERVES 6

15ml olive oil
1 onion, finely chopped
2 cloves garlic, chopped
250g smoked bacon, chopped
1 red pepper, diced
1 green pepper, diced
1 yellow pepper, diced
15ml mild curry powder
500ml cooked basmati rice
30ml fresh thyme, removed
from stem and chopped
salt and freshly ground
black pepper

METHOD

Heat the oil in a large pan and sauté the onion and garlic for 2 minutes until soft. Add the bacon and cook until slightly crispy. Add the peppers and cook for another 2 minutes.

Add the curry powder and cook for a further 30 seconds. Add the cooked rice and thyme and stir until combined. Season to taste and serve warm.

Siba's tip...
Be sure to cook the rice before making the bacon and veggie mixture. Also don't overcook the rice as it needs to be loose and fluffy rather than sticky and stodgy.

HERBED MUSHROOM TIN LOAVES

Bread baked in tins is such a South African thing, as is steaming bread in an enamel dish to make idombolo, as we call it. So, while this recipe is inspired by tradition, it has a modern flavour and is quick to make as it doesn't require the proofing that yeast bread does. The beer, apart from giving it flavour, acts as a kind of raising agent along with the baking powder, and the alcohol evaporates during baking. It's delicious with cream cheese.

PREPARATION TIME: 10 MIN
COOKING TIME: 30-35 MIN
MAKES 2 TINS OF BREAD

30ml butter
½ onion, diced
2 cloves garlic, crushed
3 large (120g) portobello mushrooms
1 green pepper, cored and diced
20ml soy sauce
35ml fennel, chopped with stems off
35ml parsley, chopped

BREAD
260ml self-raising flour
280ml brown bread flour
5ml salt
3ml baking powder
125ml cold beer or cold soda water

CHIVE CREAM CHEESE
60-80ml cream cheese
20ml onion or garlic chives, chopped
5ml lemon juice
1 spring onion, very finely chopped,
including the green part
pinch of salt, to taste

METHOD

Preheat the oven to 180°C and lightly grease two clean cans (washed 400g baked bean, tomato or similar) with cooking spray. Heat the butter and sauté the onion and garlic for 2 minutes. Add the mushrooms and cook for another 2–3 minutes, then add the green pepper for a minute and season with soy sauce. Remove from the heat, stir in the herbs and cool.

In a large bowl, mix the flour, salt and baking powder. Then make a well in the centre. Pour the beer into the well and stir with a wooden spoon.

Now lightly knead the dough that has formed. Divide the dough into two, and flatten to form an oblong shape, as wide as the tin is high. Spread the mushroom mixture over the surface and roll up the flattened dough. Transfer to the prepared tins and place on a baking tray for steadiness. Bake for 30–35 minutes, until cooked and slightly golden.

Remove from the tins as soon as possible and place on a cooling rack to cool down slightly. Cut into slices and place on a serving board. Mix the cream cheese spread ingredients together, place in a small bowl and serve with the bread.

Siba's tip...
The tins must be the old-fashioned ones that need to be opened with a tin opener as the pull-open tops leave a rim inside the tin that the baked bread will get stuck on when being removed. The oven rack must be one lower than the middle one so that the tins aren't too close to the top element. The breads should be removed as soon as possible because if they cool down inside the tins they'll sweat and become soggy.

IS A XHOSA NAME FOR THE SOFT
PORRIDGE MADE OF MAIZE MEAL
THAT'S EATEN FOR BREAKFAST.
IT CAN ALSO REFER TO A STIFFER
CONSISTENCY OF MAIZE MEAL
PORRIDGE, CALLED PAP, EATEN AS
PART OF A SAVOURY MEAL THAT
CAN INCLUDE RED MEAT, SPINACH
OR WILD LEAVES (ALSO KNOWN AS
MORORGO) AS WELL AS GRAVY OR
A TOMATO RELISH-LIKE SOUP THAT
WE CALL ISISHEBO.

MFINO FRITTERS WITH SOY MAYO + SALMON

MFINO IS A TYPE OF TRADITIONAL FOOD I GREW UP EATING AS A CHILD, ESPECIALLY IN SUMMER. MY MOTHER USED TO MAKE IT AS A MIDDAY SNACK FOR US TO HAVE ON OUR WAY BACK FROM SCHOOL. IT'S TYPICALLY EATEN BY WOMEN RATHER THAN MEN AND IS MADE OF SAUTÉED ONIONS, SPINACH AND MAIZE MEAL AND SEASONED WITH SALT. ONCE COOKED IT CRUMBLES AND IS USUALLY EATEN BY HAND. WHEN I HAD MY FIRST BORN, LONWABO, MY MOTHER CAME TO CAPE TOWN TO SEE THE BABY, AND MADE MFINO FOR ME. THE NEXT DAY I PLAYED AROUND WITH THE LEFTOVERS IN THE KITCHEN AND CAME UP WITH THESE DELICIOUS MFINO FRITTERS. THEY REALLY HAVE A TASTE OF AFRICA, BUT WITH A BIT OF A GLOBAL TOUCH!

PREPARATION TIME: 10 MIN
COOKING TIME: 20 MIN
SERVES 4–6

30ml olive oil
½ red onion, finely chopped
2 spring onions, chopped
2 cloves garlic, finely crushed
200g spinach, washed, stalks removed and finely chopped
45ml coriander, chopped
30ml thyme, chopped
170ml maize meal
salt and freshly ground black pepper

TOPPING
60ml thick mayonnaise
20ml soy sauce
5ml lemon zest
1 fillet Norwegian smoked salmon
micro herbs, to garnish

METHOD

In a large frying pan, heat the oil and sauté the red onion, spring onions and garlic for 1 minute. Add the spinach and herbs and cook for another minute or two until the spinach starts to wilt.

Stir in the maize meal and mix. Pour in 60ml water, season with salt and pepper and stir to combine until the spinach is wilted and the maize meal is slightly cooked and looking a bit like mashed potato. This takes about 10–15 minutes. Remove from the heat and allow to cool enough to handle.

Use a teaspoon scoop, and your hands, to shape the maize mixture into mini balls. Then squeeze them firmly – so that they won't break apart when you fry them – and flatten them slightly. Place a knob of butter in a heated non-stick pan, and cook them for 1 minute on each side, until golden. Place on a serving platter.

Now mix the mayo, soy sauce and zest together. Place a small dab on each fritter and top with a piece of smoked salmon. Decorate with micro herbs.

Siba's tip...
I often make these fritters as part of a finger food menu for friends and special guests. They're also great as canapés for a party. You can use polenta instead of maize meal, but just make sure you add enough polenta to prevent the mixture from being too soft to form into shape. It must also be flexible enough to shape into small round balls.

GRILLED PAPCAKES

MAIZE MEAL IS A MUCH-LOVED AFRICAN STAPLE THAT WE GREW UP EATING, AND WHILE IT TASTES GREAT AS IS, I FIND IT TAKES VERY LITTLE EFFORT TO MAKE IT TASTE DELICIOUS. I LOVE INFUSING IT WITH HERBS AND IT REALLY WORKS WELL WITH BACON. THESE PAPCAKES ARE MADE IN A SIMILAR WAY TO THE MFINO FRITTERS BUT ARE BIGGER, AND BEST SERVED WITH BRAAIED MEAT OR BOEREWORS AND SALSA.

METHOD

PREPARATION TIME: 10 MIN
COOKING TIME: 20 MIN
SERVES 4

1 litre cold water
15ml chicken stock powder
2ml salt
375ml maize meal
30ml butter

MIX WITH
250g bacon rashers, chopped
1 onion, chopped
2 cloves garlic, crushed
30ml parsley, chopped
30ml coriander, chopped
sea salt and freshly ground
black pepper, to taste

In a saucepan, mix the water with the chicken stock powder and salt, and bring to the boil. Whisk in the maize meal, adding a little at a time and whisking continuously to prevent lumps forming.

Now stir with a wooden spoon, mashing the pap against the sides of the saucepan to prevent lumps from forming. Reduce the heat to medium, cover and cook for 15 minutes. Stir again and cook for another 10 minutes, until cooked.

Dry fry the bacon in a large non-stick pan until crispy and set aside. Using the rendered fat, sauté the onion and garlic for 3–4 minutes. Add the herbs and stir. Now add the herbed onion mixture and crispy bacon to the pap and stir to combine.

Transfer to a baking pan and press down until even. Cut into round shapes using cookie cutters and brush each cake with melted butter.

Heat a griddle pan and grill the papcakes for 2–3 minutes or so on each side until charred lines are visible, before setting them aside.

Siba's tip...
It's totally fine for the bottom of the pap to form a tortilla-like hard shell and leave the pan clean underneath, once removed. As kids we used to add jam to this and have it as a snack.

PAPIZZA

I created this recipe many years ago in my food editor days. I wanted to make pizza but realized I had run out of pizza base. Raiding my cupboards, I came across maize meal and it sparked an idea. I created a pizza base with cooked maize meal and my family lapped it up. I have since made many variations of it, but this is one of my favourites.

PREPARATION TIME: 10 MIN
COOKING TIME: 40 MIN
SERVES 4

750ml water
pinch of salt
530ml maize meal
30ml butter
125ml basil or rocket pesto (see recipe on page 157)
30ml sweet chili sauce
225g chorizo, sliced
½ red onion, sliced
150g broccolini, blanched
300ml Parmesan, shaved
sea salt and freshly ground black pepper, to taste

METHOD

Preheat the oven to 220°C. In a medium-sized saucepan, bring the water and salt to a rapid boil. Add half the maize meal and whisk to remove any lumps. Reduce the heat to medium, stir with a wooden spoon and cook, covered, for 8 minutes.

Stir the mixture again and add the remaining maize meal, a little at a time, stirring and repeatedly mashing it against the sides of the saucepan with the back of the wooden spoon to prevent lumps from forming. This should take about 5 minutes.

Reduce the heat further, cover and cook for 15–20 minutes until the pap has thickened to a stiff consistency and is cooked. Add the butter and mix. Cool slightly. Flatten the cooled pap into a pizza pan to create a thin base.

Smear the base with half the pesto and all of the sweet chili sauce. Scatter the chorizo, onion, broccolini, spoonfuls of the remaining pesto and Parmesan cheese. Season to taste and bake for 10 minutes, or until the cheese has melted. Serve warm, in pizza-like slices.

Siba's tip...
You'll need a pizza lifter or fish slicer to lift the slices as the pappiza will be soft when warm. To blanch the broccolini, bring salted water to the boil. Add the broccolini for 2 minutes, then remove and place in a colander before rinsing with cold water to refresh the colour, and draining.

MOROGO

VETKOEK / AMAGWINYA

FRIED DOUGH ROLLS THAT ARE CALLED FAT CAKES IN ENGLISH. THEY'RE A VERY POPULAR FOOD ESPECIALLY IN THE TOWNSHIPS, AND ARE QUITE OFTEN SOLD IN A CORNER SPAZA SHOP ACCOMPANIED EITHER BY POLONY, MINCED CURRY OR FISH CAKES. THEY'RE OFTEN SERVED AS A SUBSTITUTE FOR BREAD AND CAN BE EATEN AS THEY ARE. THEIR NON-FRIED, PAN GRILLED COUSIN IS CALLED INGSTLE IN XHOSA AND ROOSTERKOEK IN AFRIKAANS

NAARTJIE   AT...

AN AFRIKAANS WORD FOR A CITRUS FRUIT THAT'S ALMOST LIKE THE SIZE OF AN ORANGE AND HAS LOOSE AND EASY-TO-PEEL SKIN. IT'S SIMILAR TO A TANGERINE, SATSUMA AND MANDARIN, BUT A LITTLE SWEETER AND HAS A WIDELY TART CITRUS TASTE.

MOPANI WORMS ALSO KNOWN AS MASONJA

SIMILAR TO CATERPILLARS AND NAMED AFTER THE MOPANI TREES THEY MAINLY INHABIT. THEY'RE POPULAR IN THE NORTHERN PROVINCE WITH THE SHANGAAN, VHENDA AND BAPEDI PEOPLE. THEY'RE HAND-PICKED AND THE INSIDES ARE SQUEEZED OUT AND SUN DRIED ON ROOFTOPS (TO PRESERVE THEM). THEY CAN BE EATEN AS THEY ARE; DRIED AS A SNACK OR REHYDRATED WITH WATER AND COOKED WITH ONIONS AND TOMATOES AND SERVED WITH PAP.

ULUSU / MALA MOGODU

BOTH OF THESE NAMES REFER TO TRIPE, WHICH IS USUALLY SERVED WHEN THERE'S A SPECIAL CELEBRATION, SUCH AS A TRADITIONAL WEDDING OR THE HOMECOMING OF YOUNG MEN FROM INITIATION SCHOOL. IT OFTEN INVOLVES THE SLAUGHTERING OF COWS OR SHEEP, AND IS CUSTOMARILY CLEANED BY THE WOMEN, WITH HELP FROM THE KIDS. IT'S THEN COOKED IN BIG POTS WITH JUST SALTED WATER FOR A COUPLE OF HOURS UNTIL VERY TENDER, AND SERVED FOR BREAKFAST OR LUNCH WITH STEAMED BREAD (IDOMBOLO) OR PAP.

INYAMA

A XHOSA WORD THAT REFERS TO MEAT. INYAMA EBOMVU IS RED MEAT AND INYAMA YENKUKHU IS CHICKEN.

BRAAI / SHISA NYAMA

AMASI / 'MAAS' / SOUR MILK

TRADITIONALLY MADE FROM UNPASTEURISED MILK THAT'S LEFT TO FERMENT IN A CALABASH. COMMERCIALLY SOLD AMASI TASTES AND LOOKS LIKE BUTTERMILK AND CAN BE USED IN PLACE OF IT IN MOST BAKING RECIPES. IT'S TRADITIONALLY EATEN WITH CRUMBLY MAIZE MEAL PORRIDGE THAT WE CALL UMPHOKOQO, PHUTU OR PHUMPHALANA.

CHAAR

UNRIPENED MANGO THAT'S BEEN CUT INTO CHUNKS AND PRESERVED IN SPICY OIL. IT'S STORED IN SMALL BUCKETS OR JARS AND FREELY AVAILABLE IN MOST SUPERMARKETS. IT'S EATEN AS A PICKLE OR SALAD AND NOT IN EXCESS AS IT'S KNOWN TO TRIGGER AN OFFENSIVE ARMPIT SMELL. IT WAS IMPORTED TO SOUTH AFRICA BY INDIAN MIGRANTS.

ROOIBOS

AN AFRIKAANS WORD, MEANING RED BUSH, WHICH REFERS TO THE ROOIBOS PLANT AND THE TEA MADE BY INFUSING ITS LEAVES. IT HAS A POPULAR, EARTHY TASTE AND MANY HEALTH BENEFITS DUE TO BEING CAFFEINE-FREE AND FULL OF MINERALS AND ANTIOXIDANTS. IT'S A WELL-KNOWN SOUTH AFRICAN EXPORT AND AVAILABLE AS TEA ALL OVER THE WORLD.

BILTONG

RAW, SALTED AND SPICED MEAT THAT'S TRADITIONALLY AIR DRIED. IT'S MAINLY MADE FROM BEEF, THOUGH OSTRICH, KUDU AND OTHER TYPES OF RED MEAT ARE ALSO USED AND, NOWADAYS, EVEN CHICKEN AND BACON. IT'S VERY SIMILAR TO AMERICAN BEEF JERKY, AND MOSTLY SOLD IN THIN SLICES.

UMNGQUSHO / SAMP + BEANS

UMNGQUSHO IS THE XHOSA WORD FOR A TRADITIONAL SAMP AND BEAN DISH, USING RED SPECKED SUGAR BEANS, SOME FORM OF FAT OR OIL AND SPICES. IT'S OFTEN SERVED FOR SUPPER WITH BEEF OR LAMB MEAT STEW.

A SOTHO AND TSWANA WORD FOR WILD LEAVES THAT GROW FREELY, WITHOUT BEING PLANTED. THEY INCLUDE PUMPKIN LEAVES AND BEETROOT TOPS, AND CAN REFER TO RAW OR COOKED SPINACH TOO. MOROGO IS ALSO THE NAME OF A TRADITIONAL SOUTH AFRICAN DISH MADE FROM WILD LEAVES AND SAUTÉED ONIONS AND GOES BY DIFFERENT NAMES IN DIFFERENT REGIONS. IN THE EASTERN CAPE WE CALL THEM UMFINO.

GATSBY

A BAGUETTE-LIKE 'SANDWICH' THAT'S A POPULAR LUNCHTIME TAKE-AWAY SNACK, PARTICULARLY IN THE CAPE FLATS WHERE IT ORIGINATES. IT'S SOLD FOOT LONG WITH A VARIATION OF STUFFINGS, SUCH AS MASALA STEAK STRIPS, FRIED CALAMARI SAUSAGES, POLONY AND ALWAYS CHIPS INSIDE TOO. IT SOMETIMES COMES WITH DIFFERENT SAUCE OPTIONS.

SKOP / SMILEY

A SHEEP'S HEAD THAT'S BEEN THOROUGHLY CLEANED BY HAVING ITS HAIR BURNT OFF OVER THE FIRE AND THEN SCRUBBED AND RINSED. IT'S THEN CUT IN HALF LENGTHWAYS, THROUGH THE EYES AND NOSE, AND CLEANED AGAIN, ESPECIALLY IN THE NOSE AND EARS. IT'S THEN COOKED IN SALTED WATER FOR HOURS, UNTIL IT BECOMES SOFT AND THE MEAT FLESH HAS SHRUNK. WHEN THIS HAPPENS, ITS TEETH SHOW, HENCE THE NAME SMILEY. IT'S A TOWNSHIP DELICACY AND VERY POPULAR AMONGST MEN AS A SNACK, BOTH ON ITS OWN AND WITH PAP. IT'S ALSO SOLD AS STREET FOOD, EITHER WRAPPED IN NEWSPAPER OR A PLASTIC BAG.

BRAAI IS AN AFRIKAANS WORD REFERRING TO OPEN-AIR GRILLING OR BARBECUING, USING WOOD OR CHARCOAL. IT'S A POPULAR WAY OF ENTERTAINING WHEN FRIENDS COME TOGETHER. CHOPS, ESPECIALLY LAMB AND PORK, WITH BOEREWORS ARE USUALLY ACCOMPANIED BY CORN AND CHAKALAKA. ANOTHER WELL-KNOWN TERM THAT ALSO REFERS TO BRAAING, IN ZULU, IS SHISA NYAMA. THIS CAN ALSO APPLY TO A POPULAR BUTCHERY WITH A BRAAING SPOT, SUCH AS MZOLI'S BUTCHERY, WHICH IS VERY POPULAR IN CAPE TOWN. SHISA NYAMA IN EAST AFRICA IS CALLED NYAMA CHOMA.

MEALIE-MEAL

MEALIE IS THE AFRIKAANS WORD FOR MAIZE (CORN), SO MEALIE-MEAL REFERS TO MAIZE MEAL OR CORN MEAL. IT'S MADE FROM THE WHITE MAIZE VARIETY AND HAS A COURSE TEXTURE. MEALIE-MEAL IS A POPULAR STAPLE, ESPECIALLY AMONG THE ETHNIC SOUTH AFRICAN GROUPS AND THROUGHOUT AFRICA (THOUGH NOT IN NORTH AFRICA). IT'S WHAT PAP (STIFF MAIZE MEAL PORRIDGE) IS MADE FROM AND IS QUITE SIMILAR TO ITALIAN POLENTA AND AMERICAN GRITZ, ONLY THESE ARE MADE FROM THE YELLOW MAIZE VARIETY. PAP IS OFTEN SERVED FOR SUPPER WITH MEAT AND VEGETABLES, BUT IT'S ALSO POPULAR AS A SOFT MORNING PORRIDGE, GOING BY DIFFERENT NAMES SUCH AS ISIDUDU, IPHALISHI AND LESHELESHELE. IT'S SERVED WITH BUTTER AND A SPRINKLING OF SUGAR AND MILK, AND I EVEN REMEMBER ADDING BLOBS OF PEANUT BUTTER. PAP GOES BY DIFFERENT NAMES IN DIFFERENT COUNTRIES, SUCH AS SADZA IN ZIMBABWE, NSIMA IN MALAWI AND ZAMBIA, AND UGALI IN UGANDA.

BUCHU

A NATIVE SOUTH AFRICAN BUSH WITH A STRONG AROMATIC SMELL. THE NAME COMES FROM THE KHOISAN WORD, BOOKOO, WHICH MEANS DUSTING POWDER. AN INFUSION OF THE LEAVES BRINGS ABOUT A STIMULATING AND SOOTHING EFFECT ON THE URINARY SYSTEM.

PINEAPPLE COOLER

OH, I HAVE SUCH GREAT MEMORIES OF THIS DRINK! IT'S A SUMMER DRINK WE USED TO MAKE AS KIDS WITH MY BROTHER VIWE AND OUR COUSINS. MY MOTHER TAUGHT US HOW TO MAKE IT AND SHE WOULD ALWAYS WARN US NOT TO ADD ANY YEAST AS IT FERMENTS AND TURNS INTO ALCOHOL. THIS, OF COURSE, IS EXACTLY WHY WE WOULD ADD THE YEAST AND BE DELIGHTED BY IT. FORTUNATELY, IT WOULD NEVER FERMENT LONG ENOUGH TO BECOME AN ALCOHOLIC BEVERAGE AS WE WOULD ALWAYS DIG IN TOO SOON.

PREPARATION TIME: 10 MIN
NO COOKING TIME
WAITING TIME: 24-48 HRS
MAKES 1,5L

2 fresh pineapples, scrubbed
15ml instant yeast
200ml white sugar
1,5 litres lukewarm water

SERVE WITH
1 lemon, cut in slices (optional)
1 pineapple, peeled and cut
into pieces
a few raspberries, to garnish

METHOD

Remove the stems from the pineapples and discard. Peel off the skins with a sharp knife and keep the pineapple flesh in the fridge until needed.

Now, in a large jug or bucket, place the pineapple skin with the yeast and sugar. Cover with lukewarm water and stir continuously to dissolve the sugar. Cover with plastic wrap and a tea towel, and leave in a warm place to ferment for between 24 and 48 hours.

Strain the fermented pineapple mixture through a clean muslin cloth placed inside a strainer. Discard the pineapple peels and other solids, and chill in the fridge. When ready to serve, pour into glasses. Top with lemon slices, pineapple pieces and raspberries, and enjoy!

SCAN TO WATCH
A VIDEO ON
HOW TO
MAKE THIS RECIPE

Siba's tip...

I often make this for picnics with my family. I pour it into two or three 500ml bottles, leaving enough space at the top to add fresh fruit pieces, and then freeze them overnight. On the day of the picnic, I pack them in my basket near the salads to keep everything chilled, and they defrost on the way. Just before serving, I add the pineapple pieces and raspberries. Since it takes some time to make, you may want a bigger yield, in which case feel free to double the quantities.

HOMEMADE GINGER BEER

Making ginger beer was a norm in most households during my childhood summers. As kids visiting distant family members, we could count on being served it along with what I call township scones, which are something between the English scone and a muffin. Each family has their own ginger beer recipe and swears theirs is the best. Well, I am no different thanks to this special recipe I was given by Brian's grandmother, Makhumalo. I have tweaked it a little, by adding fresh ginger for a stronger flavour and some yeast to quicken the fermentation process and produce a bubbling effect.

METHOD

PREPARATION TIME: 10 MIN
COOKING TIME: 10 MIN
WAITING TIME: 8 HRS
MAKES 4L

475ml white sugar
4 litres water
30ml ground ginger
150ml fresh ginger, grated
2ml tartaric acid
2ml cream of tartar
5ml yeast (optional)
30ml raisins

SERVE WITH
1 lemongrass stick, cut in half
a few fresh ginger slices, made with a peeler
125ml crushed ice

Heat the sugar and 250ml water in a saucepan, stirring continually until the sugar has dissolved. Add both the ground and fresh ginger, the tartaric acid and cream of tartar, and bring to a simmer.

Simmer for 10 minutes until the mixture has slightly thickened and become golden in colour. Mix the syrup with the remaining water, stir in the yeast, and transfer to a clean 4-litre bucket with a lid or two 2-litre plastic bottles. Add the raisins.

Place in a warm spot, but not in direct sunlight, for 8 hours. (If you choose to leave the yeast out, place in a warm spot for 24–48 hours, and open the bucket or bottles every 12 hours to allow the gas to escape.) The raisins should start spinning and rising to the top when the ginger beer is ready.

Strain using a clean muslin cloth, chill and add the lemon juice, if using. Serve with fresh ginger slices and lemongrass, to impart flavour, and crushed ice.

Siba's tip...
If not already bottled, the ginger beer must be bottled as soon as the raisins start spinning and surfacing. Remove those raisins when straining the ginger beer and add new ones just before chilling if you prefer. You can also flavour the ginger beer with 30–45ml of pineapple drink concentrate, adding it just before the fermentation begins, and then serving with pineapple slices.

MILK TART

Popularly referred to as melktert, this dish is a truly authentic South African one. I was given this tasty recipe in a practical class at culinary school many years ago. I've altered it slightly to make the filling lighter and more airy. If you're attempting this recipe for the first time, read the whole recipe through, along with the tip, so you know what's coming and can get certain things ready before starting. Once you've tasted it, you'll find it seriously hard to buy a store-bought milk tart again because it's that good!

PREPARATION TIME: 20 MIN
COOKING TIME: 15 MIN
BAKING TIME: 30 MIN
SERVES 6+

250ml all-purpose flour
125ml butter
60ml icing sugar
15–30ml iced cold water
(optional)

MILK CUSTARD FILLING
750ml full cream milk
1 stick cinnamon
2 whole cloves
1 cardamom seed
60ml all-purpose flour
80ml white sugar
2ml salt
30ml butter
3 eggs, separated
5ml vanilla extract

SUGAR SPRINKLE
5ml ground cinnamon
2ml nutmeg, very finely
ground (optional)
30ml caster sugar

METHOD

Place the pastry ingredients in a food processor and pulse until the mixture resembles coarse breadcrumbs. Tip onto a clean surface and gather to form into a dough. Cover with plastic wrap and chill in the fridge for at least one hour.

Now preheat the oven to 180°C. Remove the dough from the fridge and place on a lightly floured surface. Dust a rolling pin with flour and gently roll the dough out. Place over a greased 23cm loose-bottom tart tin, with edges of the dough slightly higher than the tin. Chill in the fridge for 30 minutes, then prick the bottom with a fork a few times and blind bake (see tip below) it in the oven for 10 minutes until half baked. Remove from the oven.

Heat 625ml of the milk and the spices in a heavy bottomed saucepan until just below boiling point. In a small bowl, mix the flour, sugar and salt together and add the remaining milk, stirring to prevent lumps. Add to the hot milk mixture and whisk well. Cook over a low heat, stirring continuously until slightly thickened. Remove from the heat and stir in the butter. Allow to cool.

Remove the spices, beat the egg yolks (please note it's only the yolks) together with the vanilla extract, and stir into the cooled milk mixture. In a large clean bowl, whisk the egg whites until they're softly peaking and gently fold into the custard mixture. Pour into the half-baked pastry shell and bake for about 25–30 minutes until set.

Mix the sugar sprinkle ingredients together and sprinkle over the milk tart once it has cooled slightly. Serve at room temperature or chilled.

Siba's tip...
Blind baking is necessary when the filling requires less time to cook than the pastry. In this instance, half bake the pastry by covering it with baking paper and filling it with heavy ingredients like rice or beans to weigh it down and prevent it from puffing up while baking. Once half-baked, remove the beans and paper.

ULTIMATELY YOU WOULD
WANT THE DISHES TO LOOK
AND TASTE

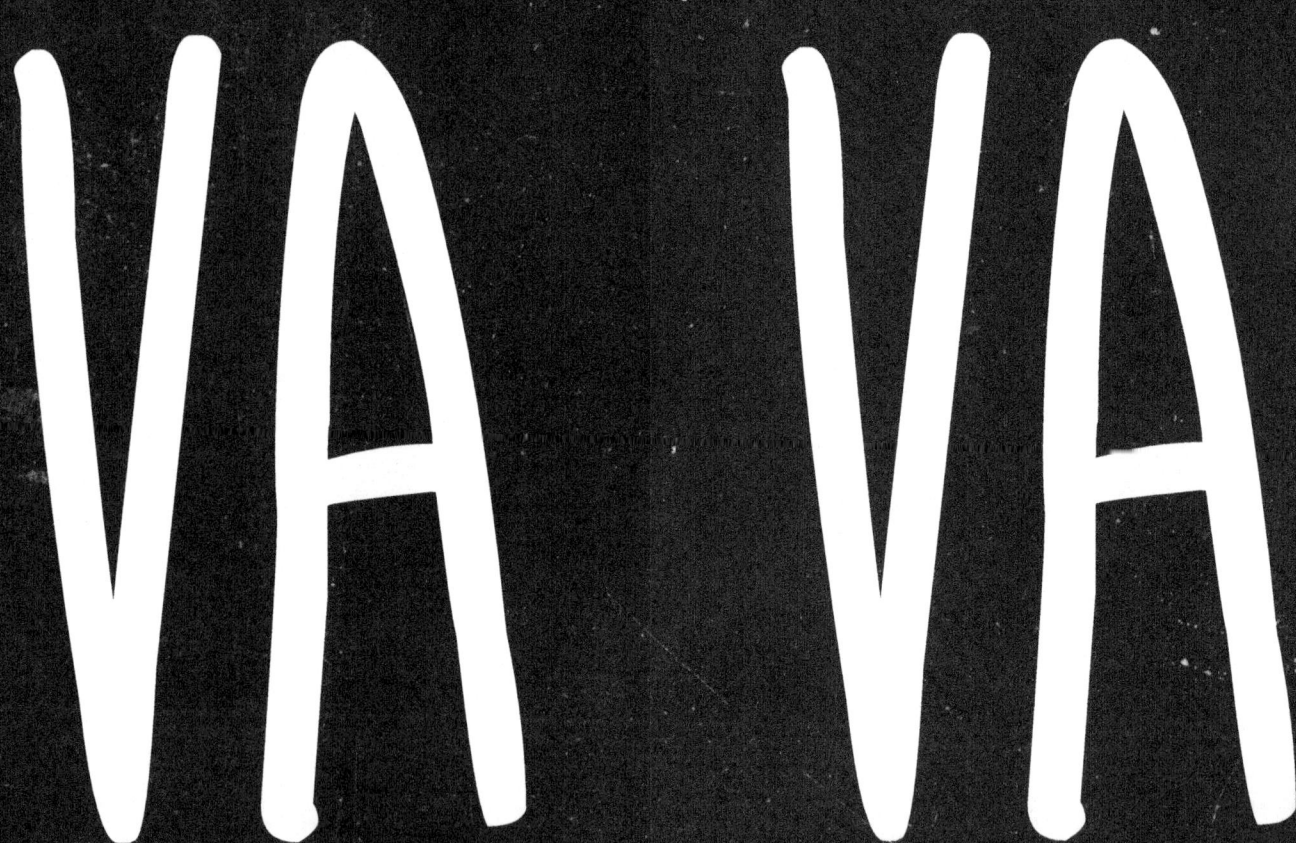

VA VA

behind the scenes.

IT INVOLVES A
LOT OF HARD WORK...

...LOADS OF
PASSION + SKILL

...AND A TALENTED TEAM

thanks everyone!

This book has been a long-held dream, further encouraged by the many, many requests from my followers. The final impetus was an email from the mom of a nine-year-old girl in the USA in November 2014. She told me that all her daughter wanted for Christmas was a copy of my book and that she'd been unable to find one anywhere. It made me realise that I could no longer avoid this daunting task. So, I want to thank my followers. You've inspired me and pushed me to realise my dream.

I could never have attempted it without the backing of my husband, Brian. His enthusiasm, practical advice and hands-on involvement have been amazing. More importantly, his emotional support kept me going when I just wanted to pull a blanket over my head. His kindly acceptance of my need to rest and escape was always balanced by a reminder that I need to soldier on. Brian, thank you from the bottom of my heart.

A special thank you goes to my dear parents, Mncedisi and Noliza Mnwana, who allowed me to follow my passion. Thank you also to Brian's parents, Alice and Peter Buys, and uncle Lungelo Mtongana, for their unwavering loyalty; and my sister Zanele Mzaca, who helps us in so many ways.

Brian and I decided to self-publish because I had an exact picture of what the book should be; and I wanted to work with a like-minded team.

This is where I have to thank God. I have prayed about this dream for so long and have always felt that He was nudging me on. He has provided what I can only call 'supernatural breaks' in bringing this project to fruition, particularly in the team members he has steered our way.

Christoph and Diane Heierli, who styled and photographed my recipes, exceeded my greatest expectations. They made my vision a reality and I am deeply grateful for that. And I'm indebted to the rest of the extremely talented production team who performed all the duties involved in publishing the book; as well as those who have been of great help to me along the way. My special thanks go to the following team members: Madeline Lass, with whom we instantly connected when we met the very first time in Johannesburg, you are absolutely amazing and I look forward to working with you on many more projects in the future. Julie Taylor, who was able to take our initial vision to the next level by capturing everything we wanted and more. Mary Duncan, who tirelessly worked on this book and has given far more than expected. Our darling friend, Michelle Liao, who used her phenomenal coordinating skills to ensure that we meet all our deadlines. Jerome Harrison, who provided great insight and advice on all print production matters. I call you all my A+ team!

These thank-yous would never be complete without mentioning Nick Thorogood and Sue Walton, former Food Network employees who discovered me. You both hold a very dear and special place in my heart – thank you for having so much faith in me. To Rachel Purnell, for the wonderful magic you create in producing Siba's Table and your unwavering support. And last but certainly not least, thanks go to Gareth Williams and the rest of the Food Network team in London, for your amazing support and the grand platform you've created across the world for me to share my love and passion for food, and for putting SA and Africa on the map!

index

This is where you'll find that recipe you need in a hurry!

First edition published 2015 by Siba Mtongana
ISBN 978-0-620-68383-8

Recipes + content **Siba Mtongana**
Creative Director + design **Brian Mtongana**
Design and repro **Julie Taylor** (AndSomeCreative)
Photographer **Christopher Heierli** (C+D photography)
Food stylist **Diane Heierli** (C+D photography)
Food assistants **Tebogo Ndala**, **Rosalind McOnie**,
Laura Cole, **Mareli Erasmus**
Kitchen assistants **Khanyo Gazi**, **Wendy Zilwa**
Hair + makeup **Nathaline Renaud**
Editor **Madeline Lass**
Copy editor **Mary Duncan**
Proofreader **Selena Abelse**
Project manager **Michelle Liao**
Production manager **Jerome Harrison**

www.sibamtongana.com

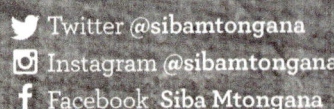

Twitter @sibamtongana
Instagram @sibamtongana
Facebook Siba Mtongana